Francisco Bruquetas

SPANISH
FOR
ENGINEERS

USING ENGLISH TO LEARN SPANISH

SPANISH FOR ENGINEERS
USING ENGLISH TO LEARN SPANISH
© 2013 Francisco de la Calle

ISBN: 978-0-578-11958-8

R150229

Cover Art: Francisco de la Calle

Bruquetas Publishing
88 S. Third St. #162, San José, California 95112, USA
www.BruquetasPublishing.com

For my parents

Foreword

In the old times -when I completed my bachelor - *ingeniería industrial* in Spain was a six-year program intended to provide the country with professionals with a strong foundation on every aspect of industry: primarily on electrical and mechanical engineering, but also on metallurgic, electronics, chemistry or production management.

Now the veteran *Escuela Superior de Ingenieros Industriales de Madrid* has become the first Spanish college to be accredited by the U.S. Accreditation Board for Engineering and Technology (ABET) and its studies of industrial engineering has given rise to more specialized (and shorter) major programs. Time has passed but that proper notion of an engineer as a generalist still remains.

Spanish for Engineers devotes chapters to specialties, paying special attention to project management in the construction sector. The vocabulary for project management is enriched with day-to-day terms from financial advisors, entrepreneurs, vendors, etc. also necessary for the engineers.

In turn, the construction projects are a good paradigm of different engineering teams interwoven. Besides, the structure and architecture, the electrical and mechanical systems, the electronic controls, or safety features need to fit in.

This book is a fresh start to learn Spanish while rediscovering words. You will learn the words that you need and grammar structures to join those words in order to create you personalized foundations in Spanish.

The Book at a Glance

SECTION IV   VERBS

APPENDICES

Table of Contents

SECTION II   WORDS

INTRODUCTION
INTRODUCCIÓN

Spanish for Engineers is intended for self-educated students with no previous knowledge of the language.

Its methodology takes advantage of the similarities between Spanish and English. Students will find motivation by realizing they are progressing, and they can speed up their learning by studying at their own pace, creating their own vocabulary, and observing sentences in clear examples. A significant percentage of English words have a Latin root, as do many structures. Spanish is derived from the Latin Language. This commonality is utilized extensively in this book to teach the Spanish language, its grammatical rules, and its coherence and consistency. For this reason, most of the Spanish words that the reader will find in this book are similar in English and, consequently, self-explanatory (as computador, control, or análisis).

The goal of this book is for professionals to be able to communicate with Spanish-speaking professionals. This book will introduce the dialogue in order to understand descriptions of data and problems, and to convey ideas and technical instructions. At the end of this book, you will be able to read and write any text, to convey most messages, and be able to understand substantial Spanish.

This textbook teaches the basics of the language, and shows how to become self-educated in Spanish: how to develop vocabulary efficiently, and how to find resources for your next-steps in the language. The book is engineered to be the perfect introduction to the complete grammar book *Spanish for Californians: Using English to Learn Spanish.*

This book sticks to what constitutes standard Spanish. Spanish is a very unified language. The rules of spelling and grammar are the same in all of the Spanish speaking countries, and twenty two National Academies, including those of the United States, Puerto Rico and the Philippines, work to maintain this unity.

The sections of the textbook correspond to goals. All languages have the same three components: a set of individual sounds, or **letters**, which are grouped to form **words**, which, in turn, are grouped to form **sentences**.

SOUNDS:	letters
VOCABULARY:	words
GRAMMAR:	sentences

Accordingly, the **sections** are:

Section I, SOUNDS, introduces and explains the elemental sounds. Spanish is very simple in terms of pronunciation and spelling; so simple that, at the end of Section I, you will be able to read in Spanish (though you won't know yet what you are saying).

Section II, WORDS, explains the rules that you need in order to learn words efficiently and expand your personal dictionary. English and Spanish have many words in common. This section shows how the words changes depending on being singular or plural, masculine or feminine, or referring to the past, present or future. These chapters show how words change their form (e.g. lion, lioness, lions, lionesses). At the end of Section II, you will be able to look up any word in the dictionary and start your own vocabulary list without mistakes.

Section III, SENTENCES, gives you the norms that you need in order to create and understand sentences. Spanish and English have many similarities in grammar. At the end of Section III, you will know how to create sentences using only three basic verb structures: "I am doing," "I have done," and "I am going to do."

Section IV, VERBS, provides additional information about the nucleus of the sentence: the verb. This section includes some verbs to give commands and instructions, as well as verbs with special characteristics.

Every chapter of the textbook will display:

- **The lesson**, with: language patterns, examples, golden rules and warnings .

- **Tips**, Frequently Asked Questions or Exercises

- **General Vocabulary**. These are words required by the language and are used in almost any circumstances. All words are sorted in alphabetical order in English in order to speed up your search.

  Words may have a mark indicating their point of stress to facilitate pronunciation. Exceptions are words as "fax" (one-vowel words) or "módem" (words with accent mark already).

  Regarding which vocabulary (technical or not) to learn, we encourage you to learn a consistent set of words per day (say, ten). Some words are required by the language, like in English "a," "the," "to," "but," etc. Other words should come from your area of interest; those are the words that should make your learning process fun. Anyway, you should wait until completing *Chapter 8 How to Learn Words Efficiently,* to learn vocabulary in a systematic fashion.

  An index of the General Vocabulary (the grammatical words) is provided at the end of the book.

- **Technical Vocabulary**. These words that are particular to your profession. These lists are also sorted in English to speed up your search, however those terms related to each other (as "asset" and "liability") are shown together.

  As in the General Vocabulary, words may have a mark indicating their point of stress to facilitate pronunciation.

  All words of the Technical Vocabulary (with the exception of those of the last chapter) are nouns. This means that they have gender. To mark this, words not ending in "o" or "a", will be preceded by "el" or "la." e.g. (el) cable, (la) construcción. An index of the General Vocabulary (the grammatical words) is provided at the end of the book.

The topics of the technical vocabulary are the following:

Chapter 1	Samples of similar words
Chapter 2	Units
Chapter 3	Specialties
Chapter 4	Specialists
Chapter 5	Construction I
Chapter 6	Construction II
Chapter 7	Materials
Chapter 8	Electricity
Chapter 9	Electronics
Chapter 10	Hardware and Software
Chapter 11	HVAC and Fire Security
Chapter 12	Mechanical Parts and Tools
Chapter 13	Project Management
Chapter 14	Accounting and Procurement
Chapter 15	Mathematics
Chapter 16	Office and Business Trips
Chapter 17	Adjetives

An index of the Technical Vocabulary is provided at the end of the book.

- **Phrasebook.** This set of translations are made with the resource of the book to facilitate self training.

- **Four appendices** supplement this book:

  APENDIX A. Notes about Dialects
  APENDIX B. Notes about Culture
  APENDIX C. Present Tense
  APENDIX D. Table of Endings of the Regular Verbs

Without further ado, here is the *Spanish for Engineers.*

SECTION I

SOUNDS
SONIDOS

In this section, you'll learn how to pronounce all of the letters in the Spanish alphabet. First, you will learn the sounds of the vowels a, e, i, o, u, and then the rest (the consonants). You will then learn the basic rules of spelling.

Later, we'll introduce "word stress," the part of the word where the emphasis falls (e.g. the "a" in actress), and its representation, the accent mark. By knowing the basic rules on the accents, you will be able to pronounce all words correctly.

By the end of this section, you will be able to read any text properly.

1. THE ALPHABET
EL ALFABETO

Spanish has the same alphabet as English, which means that they use the
same symbols (letters), and that they are sorted in the same order:

a b c d e f g h i j k l m n ñ o p q r s t u v w x y z

Spanish has only one extra letter: letter "ñ." This is placed after the letter
"n." This is the letter of words like "jalapeño" or "piñata." It sounds like
the French "gn"(e.g. co**gn**ac, filet mi**gn**on). It sounds similar to the "n" in
"onion", "bunion," or "minion; and also close to the English "nj" in
i**nj**ection).

Golden Rule

> In Spanish, each letter or pair of letters (like "ch" or "qu")
> corresponds to one sound.

For example, in Spanish, letter "a" always sounds the same (like the "a"
in father); in English, letter "a" sounds differently in "father," "cable" or
"salt."

Thus, pronouncing a word in Spanish is as simple as pronouncing its
letters one by one. For example, in Spanish, "cable" (= cable) sounds as
c + a + b + l + e (/kábleh/).

This makes Spanish one of the simplest languages in the world, and
convenient particularly for self-learners.
Sounds (or "letters," to simplify) are classified mainly by **vowels,**
represented by the letters: a, e, i, o, u; and **consonants**, the rest: b, c, d, f,

g, etc. Vowels are articulated solely by varying the openness of your mouth. The consonants require other organs: lips, teeth, tongue, palate, larynx, etc.

Other Symbols

Different symbols that you will see are: the beginning of exclamations (¡) and the beginning of questions (¿):

> Hi!   Are you Pedro?
> ¡Hola! ¿Eres Pedro?

Spanish has also a symbol to mark where the stress of the word is. In English this symbol only appears in foreign-origin words, e.g. "résumé." We'll talk about this in *Chapter 4 Accent.* For now you only need to know that all Spanish words have one, and only one, point of stress or emphasis, but this stress is not always indicated with an accent mark. This is why this book will use the underscore in those words. (e.g. ¡Hola! ¿Eres Pedro?).

Tips

Frequently Asked Question

FAQ: Why in my dictionary are "ch" and "ll" considered single letters?

> Considering "ch" and "ll" as single letters is an old rule not in use any more.

> In old dictionaries letter "ch" is placed after letter "c," and "ll" is placed after letter "l."

General Vocabulary

The names of the letters in the alphabet

Spanish is very phonetic, consequently in Spanish it is not common to spell out words. It is a good exercise to learn the alphabet though, in order to start getting familiar with the sounds (you will learn that in the next two chapters). Realize that every name of a letter has the sound of the letter, e.g. B /beh/.

Symbol	Spanish	English Pronuntiation
A	a	ah
B	be *	beh
C	ce	ceh
D	de	deh
E	e	eh
F	efe	eh-feh
G	ge	heh
H	hache	ah-cheh
I	i	ee
J	jota	ho-tah
K	ka	kah
L	ele	eh-leh
M	eme	eh-meh
N	ene	eh-neh
Ñ	eñe	eh-gneh
O	o	oh
P	pe	peh
Q	cu	koo
R	erre	eh-rreh
S	ese	eh-seh
T	te	teh
U	u	oo
V	uve *	oo-beh
W	uve doble *	oo-beh doh-bleh
X	equis	eh-kis
Y	ye *	yeh
Z	zeta	zeh-tah

(*) Other names are used, e.g. B is also called "be larga."

Technical Vocabulary

Samples of Spanish technical words that are similar in English

Since you have not learned how to pronounce the Spanish letters yet, we'll start the vocabulary section of this book with samples of words and their silmilarities with English. You will also find the words of this section in their corresponding chapter.

First, there are words English-origin words that have become part of Spanish and that are **written and pronounced as in English**. These words are *italicized* to indicate that they must be pronounced as those of the original language. Here you have some examples:

English = Spanish

byte

email

fan-coil

hardware

ipad

java

lease

newton

software

test

sprinkler

Commonly English and Spanish scientific words come from Latin (the language which Spanish comes from), and you can expect many words are similar in both languages.

A few Spanish words are **identical** to English (same spelling and pronunciation). Examples are:

English   = Spanish

blog

fax

gas

web

A few Spanish words **differ in the spelling** from their English
counterparts, but they are pronounced the same. Examples are:

English	Spanish
antenna	antena
bypass	baipás
comma	coma
modem	módem
overall	overol
scanner	escáner (*)
standard	estándar (*)

(*) In Spanish, the combination "s" followed by a consonant
     transforms into "es."

Some Spanish words differ **in the stress,** but spelling and pronunciation
are the same that their English counteparts. Examples are:

English	Spanish
metal	metal
monitor	monitor
sensor	sensor
solar	solar
vector	vector

Note: This book uses the underscore to indicate the stress.
           Also notice that, unlike English, Spanish words ending
           in "al," "ar," "or," tend to have the stress in the last
           syllable.

Some Spanish words **differ in the pronounciation** but they are spelt the
same. Examples are:

English	Spanish	
base	base	/bah-seh/
cable	cable	/kah-bleh/
gel	gel	/hel/
laser	laser	/lah-ser/
virus	virus	/bee-roos/

Most Spanish technical words that are **recognizable** from an English speaker. These words are called "cognates" in English ("cognados" in Spanish). Examples of these words are abundant.

English	Spanish
analysis	análisis
architect	arquitecto
attic	ático
column	columna
computer	computador
electricity	electricidad
pillar	pilar
plastic	plástico
proportion	proporción
ramp	rampa
sphere	esfera
telephone	teléfono
voltage	voltaje

As you will read in *Chapter 8 How to Learn Words Efficiently*, the effective vocabulary is that that comes from your experience. Only you know the words that you will use at work. At the end of each chapter you will find sets of words grouped by topics, where you can start building your own dictionary.

2. THE VOWELS
LAS VOCALES

The vowel sounds in Spanish are represented by the letters a, e, i, o, u.

Letter	Sound
a	like the "a" of father
e	like the "e" of bed
i	like the "ea" of meat
o	like the "o" of open
u	like the "oo" of boot

Use this rule of thumb to memorize the sounds: they sound in English like: ah, eh, ih, oh, uh.

Warning

Be aware that some letters, including the vowels, **don't sound identical** in both languages, but they are **close enough**. (English has a much wider range of sounds than Spanish, which gives English speakers an advantage as learners). With practice you will perfect your pronunciation.

For example, the English "oo" of "good" is slightly longer than the Spanish "u." Differences like this make the learner have an accent in Spanish. Those adjustments to the new language occur fast (and for the most part unconsciously) when trying to imitate the native speakers.

For now what is important is that you remember that the Spanish a, e, i, o, u always sound the same. On the contrary, in English, "a," for instance, sounds differently in "apple" and "ape."

Remember that every letter sounds independently. Thus, the combination of them must be pronounced accordingly. Examples:

> león = l +e + o +n (= lion)
> día = d + i +a (= day)

The letter "u" is silent when preceded by "q," or when preceded by "g." Examples:

> Quito   = k + i + t + o (= Quito)
> guitarra = g + i + t + a + r r + a ("g" like in "guitar")

Following this idea, if you have two vowels together, you must pronounce both. So, in Spanish, the name "Aaron" must sound as: a+a+r+o+n.

Tips

Exercise

Pronounce the Spanish words: Asia, cable, euro and pus (They have the same meaning in English).

When you pronounce them, if they sound like they do in English, then you did something wrong... They should sound:

> a + s + i + a
> c + a + b + l + e
> e + u + r o
> p + u + s

General Vocabulary

Numbers from 0 to 10

Symbol	Spanish Spelling	English Pronuntiation *
0	cero **	ceh-roh
1	uno	oo-noh
2	dos	dos
3	tres	tres
4	cuatro	kwa-troh
5	cinco	ceen-coh
6	seis	seh-ees
7	siete	see-eh-teh
8	ocho	oh-choh
9	nueve	nweh-beh
10	diez	dee-ehs

(*) In the next chapter, you will learn the phonetic value of the rest of the letters of the alphabet, and you will see that, in Spanish, every word is pronounced as a sequence of individual letters (sounds).

(**) As a reminder, never forget that the strongest tool that you have to memorize words in Spanish is their similarities with English. Always question yorself if the word you are going to memorize ressembles a word in English. For example, think of these words related to the table above: **tri**angle (3), **quart**er (4), **octo**pus (8), **deci**mal (10).

A single word with all vowels

There are very few words that have all the vowels. Since the vowels always sound the same (with the exception of the mute "u" in the pair "gu" and "qu"), it is worthwhile memorizing one that you can resort to when you are learning the sounds of the vowels.

An example of this is "murciélago" /moor-see-eh-lah-goh/, or simpler:

$$m + u + r + c + i + e + l + a + g + o$$

Technical Vocabulary

Units.

Units of the International System

English	Symbol	Spanish
unit		(la) **unidad** (*[1])
ampere	A	amperio (*[2])
farad	F	faradio
gram	g	gramo
kilo (kilogram)	Kg	kilo (kilogramo)
henry	H	henrio (*[3])
hertz	Hz	hercio (*[3])
joule	J	julio (*[3])
kelvin	K	(el) kelvin, grado kelvin
liter	l	litro
metro	m	metro
square meter	m^2	metro cuadrado
cubic meter	m^3	metro cúbico
centimeter	cm	centímetro
milimeter	mm	milímetro
meter per second	m/s	metro por segundo
meter per second squared	m/s^2	metro por segundo al cuadrado
newton	N	(el) *newton* (*[4])
ohm	Ω	ohmio
pascal	Pa	(el) pascal
radian	rad	(el) radián
rev. per second	rpm	(la) revolución por segundo
second	s	segundo
tonne	t	tonelada
volt	V	voltio
watt	W	vatio
kilowatt hour	KWh	kilovatio hora

Other Units (*[5])

English	Symbol	Spanish
atmosphere	atm	atmósfera
byte	B	(el) *byte*
MegaByte	MB	*Megabyte*
GigaBite	GB	*Gigabyte*
calorie	cal	caloría
decibel	dB	decibelio
degree (angle)	º	grado
degree Celsius	ºC	grado Celsius
degree Fahrenheit	ºF	grado Fahrenheit

Notes

(*[1]) In this book, only the nouns not ending in "o" or "a" have their
gender in parenthesis. As you will learn in *Chapter 6 Masculine/
Feminine*, in Spanish all nouns have gender (Nouns are the words
that defines beings and objects, as John, cat, lamp or system). As a
general rule all words ending in "o" are masculine, as "amperio."

(*[2]) Pay attention to the pronunciation of vowels explained in this
chapter. Also pay attention to the combinations of vowels, as in
amperio, cuadrado, or celsius.

(*[3]) As explained next chapter, the sound of certain consonants are
different in Spanish and English. Letter "h" is always silent. Letter
"j" is pronounced as an English "h" in Henry

(*[4]) In Spanish words in *italics* indicate that they must be pronounced in
the original language. Thus words as newton or byte must be
pronounced as in English.

(*[5]) Most Spanish-speaking countries follow the International System of
Units. US and UK units, as the ounce, pound or yard, are not used.
Below there is a lists of convertions into those units.

Conversions to U.S. units

1 g = 0.03 oz (onza de peso)

1 Kg = 2.2 Lb (libra)

1 m = 3.28 ft (el pie)

1 m = 1.094 yards (yarda)

1 cm =0.39 inch (pulgada)

1 Km = 0.62 miles (milla)

1 l = 0.26 gal (el galón); 1 l = 33.81 fl oz (onza de líquido)

1 KJ = 0.947 BTU (la unidad de energía inglesa)

3. THE CONSONANTS
LAS CONSONANTES

The consonants are those letters (sounds) that are not vowels. They are:

Letter	Sound	Examples in Spanish
b	As in English.	Bolivia
c	**Two possible sounds:**	
	When followed by *a, o, u* (ca, co, cu) or by a consonant (cr, cl) it sounds as the hard "c" in English	→ capital, coma, curioso, crema, clase (= capital, comma, curious, cream, class)
	Otherwise, it sounds like the the "c" in "**c**ement." Only in Spain, it sounds like the "th" in "**th**ing"	→ cemento, cine (= cement, cinema)
d	Softer than in English.	diamante (= diamond)
f	As in English.	Filipinas (= Philippines)
g	**Two possible sounds:**	
	1. As the guttural "g" in English, when "g" is followed by *a, o, u* (ga, go, gu, gue, gui) or a consonant (gl, gr)	→ gala, golf, gurú, guerrilla, guitarra, glándula, gris (= gala, golf, guru, guerilla, guitar, gland, gray
	2. Otherwise (ge, gi), it sounds as the "h" in "**h**ippo"	→ general, gigante (= general, giant)

Letter	Sound	Examples in Spanish
h	Silent unless combined in "ch"	hora (= hour)
j	As the English "h" in "ham, Helen, hipo or home"	San José
k	As in English	kilogramo (= kilogram)
l	As in English	lámpara (= lamp)
m	As in English	médico (= doctor)
n	As in English	Nicaragua
ñ	Like the "gn" of "cognac"	coñac (= cognac)
p	As in English	Perú
q	As is English (In Spanish, q is always followed by u)	Quito
r	**Two possible sounds:** 1. As the English "r," if not at the beginning of the word 2. At the beginning of a word, or paired, it sounds stronger (see next page)	→ hora (= hour) → rápido, carro (= rapid, car)
s	As in English	sonido (= sound)
t	As in English	Tijuana
v	As the English "b"	Venezuela
w	As in English	waterpolo (= waterpolo)
x	As in English	examen (= exam)
y	**Two possible sounds.** 1. It sounds as "ea" of "meal," when at the end of words or isolated (meaning "and") 2. Otherwise, it sounds as the English "j" in "jam"	→ y (= and), Uruguay → mayor (= major)
z	As the "c" in "cement." Only in Spain, it sounds like the English "th" in "thing"	zoología (= zoology)

Remember:

Letters b and **v** both sound like English "b."

Letter c has two sounds. In "**ce**," "**ci**," letter c sounds like in English.
Only in Spain, it sounds as the th of **th**under. Otherwise, in "**ca,
co, cu, cr, cl,**" it sounds like in English (like a "k").

Letter d is weaker than that of English. In Spanish "d" sounds especially
weak when it's placed between vowels. Thus the words
"cansado" (= tired) is pronounced "cansao" by some speakers.

Letter g has two sounds (as it does in English). In **ga, go, gu** sounds like
the g in the English **ga**rage, **go**vernment, **gu**ru. Also like
English, the combination **gue, gui** will sound: guerilla and
guitar. This very sound is the one for the combinations gl, gr,
like in gland, grand. However ge, gi sound like the Spanish "j"
of "San José," which is a stronger than the English "h" of
"ham."

Letter h is silent. However **ch** is pronounced like English of "China."

Letter ñ doesn't exist in English as a letter. However the sound is in
popular words like "piñata," "jalapeño" or "el niño" (the
atmospheric phenomenon). It sounds like the gn in co**gn**ac or
filet mi**gn**on (close to the "nj" in i**nj**ection).

Letter q can only be found in the combination with "u" to form: **que,
qui.** sounding as "k." Thus, the two spellings kilo and quilo
result in the same pronunciation.

Letter r has two pronunciations: weak and strong r (simple and multiple
vibrating r). The weak sound corresponds to that of the English
"r." The strong r is represented either by the single letter r when
in the beginning of the word or by "rr." English doesn't have
this sound. The strong r sound has the same articulation as the
weak r but the tongue vibrates (similar to the onomatopoeia
"brrr" or "grrr").

Letter y has two sounds. One as the Spanish vowel "i," (the English "ea"
of meal") when meaning "and," or when at the end of a word,
like "Paraguay." Otherwise it sounds as the English "j" in "jam."

Letter z sounds as the "c" of "ceremony". Only in Spain, it sounds as the
"th" of **th**under.

In addition, "**ch, ll, rr**" have one single sound each:

Pair	Sound	Examples in Spanish
ch	As in English.	Chile
ll	As the English "j" in joke.	llama (= flame)
rr	As the English "r," but it vibrates multiple times.	carro (= car)

Notice that only the **sounds** of the Spanish "ñ," "j," and the strong "r" are foreign in English. Try to pronounce the model words: co**gn**ac, San **Jo**sé, and "**brrr!**" Especially "**rr**" is a challenge for foreigners. Take time to learn to pronounce it.

Also notice that some letters have the same sound in Spanish. These are the pairs: b/v, ll/y, and j/g (ge, gi). These, together with the silent letter "h," become a problem of **spelling**. Examples:

> gobernar (not ~~governar~~), general (not ~~jeneral~~), fallar (not ~~fayar~~), humano (not ~~umano~~)
> (= to govern, general, to fail, human)

Regarding the pairs of consonants in the same syllable, Spanish only admits:

bl	**cl**	~~**dl**~~	**fl**	**gl**	**pl**	**tl** *
br	**cr**	**dr**	**fr**	**gr**	**pr**	**tr**

(*) Very rarely found

Notice that all of them have either "l" or "r" as the second letter of the pair.

Examples:

blusa	clon	---	Florida	glaciar	planta	nauatl
brillo	acre	dragón	Francia	gran	primer	trío

Which mean:

blouse	clone	---	Florida	glacier	plant	nauatl
brightness	acre	dragon	France	great	first	trio

Spanish doesn't have **the sounds** for the English "sh" and "sr" (sheet, Sri Lanka).

Spanish doesn't have the pair of **letters** "ck." For that **sound**, Spanish uses: "c," "qu" or "k." Spanish doen't have "ph," only "f." Examples:

> ro**ck**, che**ck**, ele**ph**ant
> ro**c**a, che**qu**e, ele**f**ante

Likewise, Spanish does not have the English pairs of **letters** bb, dd, ff, mm, pp, ss, tt or zz. For those **sounds**, Spanish uses a single letter. Examples:

> ro**bb**ery, a**dd**itional, di**ff**erence, mo**mm**y, a**pp**lication, cla**ss**,
>   lo**tt**ery, pu**zz**le
> ro**b**o, a**d**icional, di**f**erencia, ma**m**á, a**p**licación, cla**s**e,
>   lo**t**ería, pu**z**le.

Warning

> In Spanish you may find cc, mb, mp, etc., but each letter of the pair belongs to a different syllable. E.g.
>> a**c**-tor, a**c**-ci**ó**n, a-di**c**-to, e-le-fan-te
>> (= actor, action, addict, elephant)

Now, with the rules explained, you can read any word and write (maybe misspelling) any word. The only thing left to be able to read is to learn where the stress is placed on each word, which constitutes the next chapter, *Chapter 4* Accent.

Rules of Thumb on Spelling

Some basic rules can help you guess the right spelling (remember that there's no set of rules that covers all cases for the indistinguishable pairs v/b, g/j, ll/y, and the h).

> 1) Pairs "bb, dd, ff, pp, ss, tt, zz" don't exist.
> E.g. abreviación, not ~~abbreviación~~; efecto, not ~~effecto~~; adicción*, not ~~addiccion~~. (= effect; abbreviation, addiction)
> (*) Notice that the cc is, in reality, c-c, e.g. a-dic-ción

2) Words can't start with letter "s" followed by a consonant.
E.g. especial (= special), not ~~special~~ .

3) K and W are very rarely used (karate, kimono, okey –OK-, waterpolo, Washington and a few more). Use "c" or "q" for the k sound; and use: "gua, güe, güi, guo, gu" for the w-sound.

4) Use "ce," "ci," instaead of "ze," "zi."
E.g. cero, not ~~zero~~ (as in English).

5) The plural of words ending in -z, is -ces, not –zes.
E.g. cruz (= cross) → cruces, not ~~cruzes~~

6) M (not n) goes before b or p.
E.g. bomba (= bomb or pump), not ~~bomva.~~

7) Words of the same family have similar spelling.
E.g. hombre, humano, humanizar, humanidades
(= man, human, humanize, humanities)

8) Words **ending** with "i" vowel sound in Spanish are spelled:
ay, ey, oy, uy (not ai, ei, oi, ui), when the stress is not in the last vowel.
E.g. Paraguay, ahí, rey, reí, ley, leí, hoy, oí, huy, huí
(= Paraguay, there, king, I laughed, law, I read (past), today, I heard, ouch!, I fled).

9) Words starting with vowel sound "ua," "ue," "ui," "ia," and "ie" are spelled with "h:" hua, hue, hui, hia, hie.
E.g. Huáscar, huevo, huir, hiato, hielo
(= Huascar, egg, to flee, hiatus, ice).

Tips

Frequently Asked Questions

FAQ 1: Why have I never heard the English "th" sound in Spanish?

Using the "s" sound instead of "th" sound is also accepted. This use is found in Latin America, including Mexico and the US (See *Appendix A: Notes About Dialects*).

FAQ 2: What are the two dots on the "u" in "lingüista?"

Words like lingüista or pingüino (= linguist, penguin) have this
symbol called dieresis (diéresis, in Spanish). We saw that in the
combination "gue" or "gui" the "u" is silent. To spell a word
where the "u" needs to sound, you need dieresis. It is also used
in English by some newspapers to mark that a certain letter must
be pronounced, like "coöperation" (the "oo" would sound like in
boot, otherwise). Spanish uses this symbol with the same intent:
to mark that the "u" must be pronounced.

FAQ 3: I've seen both "México" and "Méjico." What's the right spelling?

Both. The Spanish words México, Nuevo México, Texas and
Oaxaca (and very few others) can be spelled with "x" or with
"j." The **Mexican** Academy of Spanish Language decided to
spell it with "x" for historical reasons. In any case, it is
pronounced as a Spanish "j" sound. In the rest of the Spanish
speaking countries, these words are spelled with "j" (Méjico,
Nuevo Méjico, Tejas, Oajaca).

FAQ 4: Should "y" and "ll" sound the same?

Originally "ll" sounded as the English "ll" in "million" (It still
sounds this way in some places in Spain and Bolivia). With
time, "ll" acquired the sound of the "y." **Nowadays** both "y"
and "ll" sound the same. On the other hand, there are variations
in the way Spanish speakers pronounce y. In Argentina, it
sounds especially strong (See *Appendix A: Notes About
Dialects*).

FAQ 5: I have heard that some people don't pronounce the "s." Is this
optional?

This is a mispronunciation. This is not standard Spanish. Every
region of the Spanish speaking world has their own "popular"
deviations from the standard. This is one: many people in the
Caribbean omit the "s" not placed at the beginning of the word.
Examples:

Standard Spanish: dos, tres, es-tó-ma-go, no-so-tros
Non Standard Spanish: do' , tre', e'tómago, no-'o-tro'
English: two, three, stomach, we

Exercises

a) Pronounce the Spanish words:

>   Puerto Rico
>   Estados Unidos (= United States)
>   California
>   Nuevo Méjico, Nuevo Méjico (same pronunciation)
>   Tejas, Texas (same pronunciation)
>   Colorado
>   Arizona
>   Nevada
>   Florida (not Florida)
>   Norteamérica (= North America)
>   Suramérica (= South America)
>   Centroamérica (= Central America)

b) Pronounce the Spanish words:

>   general (same meanings as in English: the opposite of
>   "specific" and the military rank)
>   hotel (same meaning as in English)
>   zoo (same meaning as in English)

Notes:

>   When you pronounce them, if they sound like they do in
>   English, then you are doing something wrong. They should
>   sound:
>
>   g + e+ n + e + r + a + l ("g" sounds like the "J" in "San José")
>   o + t + e + l ("h" is silent)
>   z + o + o ("z" sounds like th; "o" sounds twice)

General Vocabulary

Spanish-speaking Countries

In *Chapter 8 How to Learn Words Efficiently*, you'll have the tools to start developing your own vocabulary. Until then, you can take advantage that some names of places are the same or very similar in Spanish and English.

Remember, although words can look the same in both languages, in Spanish, they sound as letter by letter.

Spanish
Argentina
Bolivia
Chile
Colombia
Costa Rica
Cuba
República Dominicana (Dominican Republic)
Ecuador
El Salvador
Guatemala
Honduras
México/ Méjico
Nicaragua
Panamá
Paraguay
Perú
España (Spain)
Uruguay
Venezuela

Note: The countries are commonly feminine (e.g. la Argentina) feminine), however typically the article el/ la (the) is not used, consequently, you don't need to know their gender.

Technical Vocabulary

Technical specialties

English	Spanish
specialtiy	(la) especialidad
architecture	arquitectura
chemistry	química
engineering	ingeniería
aeronautical engineering	ingeniería aeronáutica
agricultural engineering	ingeniería agrícola
chemical engineering	ingeniería química
civil engineering	ingeniería civil (*[1])
electrical engineering	ingeniería eléctrica
electronic engineering	ingeniería electrónica
naval architecture	ingeniería naval
mechanical engineering	ingeniería mecánica
software engineering	ingeniería de *software* (*[2])
topography engineering	ingeniería de topografía
marketing	mercadotecnia, (el) *marketing*
mathematics	(las) matemáticas
physics	física
project management	(la) dirección de proyectos
science	ciencia
technology	tecnología

Notes
(*[1]) " ingeniería de caminos" in Spain (short for ingeniería de caminos, canales y puertos)
(*[1]) " informática

As you will learn in *Chapter 6 Masculine/ Feminine*, all Spanish nouns have gender. As a general rule, all words ending in "a" are feminine, as "arquitectura," or "quiímica" In this book, words following this rule don't have the indication "la," e.g. la especialidad

4. ACCENT
ACENTO

So far, you know how to pronounce the sound of a word but not the right intonation of it. It's not the same to say "dess<u>er</u>t" and "d<u>e</u>sert," or <u>i</u>mport and imp<u>or</u>t. Every word has a point of emphasis or stress.

All Spanish words have one and only one point of stress, and this always falls on a vowel, never on a consonant, e.g. (underscored)

> r<u>a</u>mpa, c<u>e</u>lda, m<u>i</u>lla, t<u>o</u>rre, col<u>u</u>mna
> ramp, cell, mile, tower, column

Spanish uses the accent mark (á, é, í, ó, ú) to indicate where the stress is.

> plástico, apéndice, índice, módem, número
> plastic, appendix, index, modem, number

Although all words have a point of stress, not all words have an accent mark, as you can see in the first series above: <u>a</u>sma, v<u>e</u>na, digest<u>i</u>vo, abd<u>o</u>men, vac<u>u</u>na.

This book uses the underline to indicate where the stress of a word is when the accent mark is not used.

Golden Rule

> All words, with no exception, have one, and only one, point of **stress**, and this always falls on a vowel (never on a consonant). The **accent marks** (á, é, í, ó, ú) indicate where the stressed vowel is. However, the majority of words don't require an **accent mark**.

Notice that many Spanish words that look similar to English, have a different point of stress:

> hospital, teléfono, algoritmo, televisión, único
> hospital, telephone, algorithm, television, unique

Rule of Thumb on Stress

There is a rule to help you know where the stress is when you read a word: all words that have the stress in the third to last syllable or before that must have an accent mark. Examples:

> válvula, e-léc-tri-co, quí-mi-ca, e-lec-tró-ni-co, a-cús-tico*
> valve,   electric,   chemistry, electronic,   acoustic
>
> (*) dashes above are to indicate the breakdown into syllables

In addition to this, the majority of words in Spanish have the stress in the second to last syllable.

If you combine both (the actual rule and the tendency), the resulting rule of thumb is: if a word doesn't have an accent mark, it **most likely** has the stress in the second to last syllable. Example:

> ca-rro, re-gla, ac-ci-den-te, con-te-ni-do, nor-ma, pin-tu-ra
> car,   rule,   accident,   content,   norm,   paint

Tips

Frequently Asked Questions

FAQ 1: Vídeo or Video?

> A few words can be pronounced with different stress. This is the
> case of vídeo/ vid<u>e</u>o (= video, video tape, DVR). In Mexico
> vid<u>e</u>o is preferred.
>
> Another word is período/peri<u>o</u>do (= period). You choose.

FAQ 2: What is the difference between accent mark and stress?

> Stress is the elevation of intonation of a vowel in the word. An
> accent mark is the mark that indicates that stress. In Spanish,
> every word has one (and only one) stressed vowel; however,
> most of the words don't have an accent mark. The term "accent"
> is confusing since it may mean either "stress" or "accent mark."
> Normally "accent" refers to "accent mark."
>
> This book uses the underline to mark the stress in those words
> that have no accent mark.

FAQ 3: Do I need to learn the rules for the accent marks?

> Yes and no. You need to if you want to know where the stress is
> in any word in the dictionary; in order to communicate in a
> written form, you don't need it. Any Spanish reader will
> understand your written notes without accent marks.

FAQ 4: I have seen the word "él" and "el," so the same word with and
without accent mark. Which one is correct?

> The accent mark is also used to distinguish words that have the
> same pronunciation and spelling but that can be ambiguous. So,
> "él" means "he," in English, and "el," "the". Other example is
> "sí" (= yes) , and "si" (=if).
>
> There is just a few words that have accent for this reason. The
> majority of words that have more than one meaning are not
> distinguished with the accent mark, e.g. hoja (= leaf, paper).

General Vocabulary

Interjections and greetings

English	Spanish
Excuse me.	Con permiso./ Perdón.
Good afternoon (until dusk).	Buenas tardes.
Good evening. / Good night.	Buenas noches.
Good morning (until lunch time).	Buenos días.
Goodbye.	Adiós.
Hello.	Hola.
Help!	¡Ayuda!
I don't know.	No lo sé./ No sé.
I wish!	Ojalá.
I'm sorry.	Lo siento.
Maybe.	Tal vez./ Quizás./ Quizá.
Me neither.	Yo tampoco.
Me too.	Yo también.
Okay.	Okey.
Please.	Por favor.
Really?	¿De verdad?
Right?	¿Verdad?
See you later.	Hasta la vista.
See you later.	Hasta luego.
See you soon.	Hasta pronto.
Thank you.	Gracias.
Thank you very much.	Muchas Gracias.
You're welcome.	De nada.

Technical Vocabulary

Specialists and positions

English	Spanish
specialist	especialista
position	puesto
accountant	(el/ la) contable, contador/a
analyst	(el/ la) analista
architect	arquitecto/a
client	(el/ la) cliente
competitor	competidor/a
consultant	consultor/a
contractor	(el/ la) contratista
coordinator	coordinador/a
vendor	vendedor/a, (el/ la) comercial
designer	diseñador/a
director	director/a
draftsman	(el/ la) delineante, (el/ la) proyectista
electrician	(el/ la) electricista
employee	empleado/a
engineer	ingeniero/a
foreman	(el/ la) capataz
inspector	inspector/a
manager	director/a
mechanical	mecánico/a
plumber	fontanero/a, plomero/a
president	presidente/a
professional	(el/ la) profesional
project coordinator	coordinador/a de proyectos
project manager	director/a de proyectos
site manager	jefe/a de obra
technician	(el/ la) técnico
worker	trabajador/a

Notes

In this book the undescore indicates the point of stress. Words
with just one vowel or with an accent mark won't need this help.

As you will learn in *Chapter 6: Masculine/ Feminine*, Spanish nouns they all have gender. Thus, the word "gato" (=cat) uses the masculine article "el," el gato (=the cat), no matter the real gender of the cat; and "lámpara" (= lamp) is feminine in Spanish and uses the feminine article "la lámpara," (= the lamp).

With most of the professions, as "ingeniero" or "arquitecto," you will put "o" or "a" at the end, and will use "el" or "la" if the person in question is a man or a woman:

> He is the engineer. / She is the engineer.
> Él es el ingeniero./ Ella es la ingeniera.

With professions ending in "a", as "electricista" or "especialista," the same word works for both, and you just have to put "el" or "la" accordingly.

> He is the electrician. / She is the electrician.
> Él es el electricista. / Ella es la electricista.

SECTION II

WORDS
PALABRAS

Congratulations! Now you can read and write words in Spanish.

This section will teach you how to learn the meaning of those words by looking in the dictionary. Obvious? Not really. Imagine that you want to know the meaning of the English word "appendices" (not appendix). If the dictionary doesn't include the plural of words, you would get frustrated by finding "appendix," but not "appendices."

Another example would be if you wanted to look up the English word "studied" (not: study).

This short Section II will give you a guide by discussing three topics:

> Singular/plural, also called number

> Masculine/feminine, also called gender

> Person and tense, also called conjugation

In the end of this section, you will be able to find any word in the dictionary to create your own dictionary with your own vocabulary.

5. SINGULAR / PLURAL
SINGULAR / PLURAL

Like English, Spanish has "singular/plural" (identifiers for one/more than one), and both languages use the same way to identify "more than one:" they add the letter "**s**."

Like in English if the noun is plural, then the word that precedes it (determiner) is also plural. The words "a," "the," "this," and "that" are called determiners.

a   hotel,   some   hotels
DET. NOUN   DET.   NOUN

un   hotel,   unos   hoteles
DET. NOUN   DET.   NOUN

this cat, these cats
este gato, estos gatos

that elephant, those elephants
ese elefante, esos elefantes

Unlike English, the determiner "the" also changes.

the planet, the planets
el planeta, los planetas

Unlike English, in Spanish if the noun is plural, the adjective (like elegant, black or enormous) is also plural.

an elegant hotel,
DET. ADJ. NOUN

un   hotel elegante,
DET. NOUN ADJ.

some elegant hotels,
DET.   ADJ.   NOUN

unos hoteles elegantes
DET.   NOUN   ADJ.

this black cat, these black cats (the word black does not change).
este gato negro, estos gatos negros

that enormous elephant, those enormous elephants
ese elefante enorme, esos elefantes enormes

Golden Rule

Like English, Spanish creates the plural by adding:
-"**s**," if the word ends in a vowel
-"**es**," if the word ends in a consonant

Examples

One hour, two hours, three hours
Una hora, dos horas, tres horas

One album, two albums, three albums
un álbum, dos álbum**es**, tres álbum**es**

If the word ends in letter "z," then you change "z" to a "c" and add "es."

One cross, two cros**ses**, three crosses
Una cruz, dos cru**ces**, tres cru**ces**

Only some determiners add "**os**" to create the plural. These are:

un / unos (a/some)
el / los (the/the -plural)
este / estos (this/these)
ese / esos (that/those)
aquel / aquellos (that/those)
algún / algunos (any/some)

Numbers

By paying attention to the series of numbers, you can easily deduce how
to form any figure:

1	2	3	4	5	6	7	8	9	10
uno	dos	tres	cuatro	cinco	seis	siete	ocho	nueve	diez

Note: underscore indicates stressed vowel.

10, 11, 12...19	20, 21, 22...29	30, 31, 32...39
diez	veinte	treinta
once	veintiuno	treinta y uno
doce	veintidós	treinta y dos
trece	veintitrés	treinta y tres
catorce	veinticuatro	treinta y cuatro
quince	veinticinco	treinta y cinco
dieciséis	veintiséis	treinta y seis
diecisiete	veintisiete	treinta y siete
dieciocho	veintiocho	treinta y ocho
diecinueve	veintinueve	treinta y nueve

40, 41, 42...49	50, 51, 52...59	60, 61, 62...69
cuarenta	cincuenta	sesenta
cuarenta y uno	cincuenta y uno	sesenta y uno
cuarenta y dos	cincuenta y dos	sesenta y dos
cuarenta y tres	cincuenta y tres	sesenta y tres
cuarenta y cuatro	cincuenta y cuatro	sesenta y cuatro
cuarenta y cinco	cincuenta y cinco	sesenta y cinco
cuarenta y seis	cincuenta y seis	sesenta y seis
cuarenta y siete	cincuenta y siete	sesenta y siete
cuarenta y ocho	cincuenta y ocho	sesenta y ocho
cuarenta y nueve	cincuenta y nueve	sesenta y nueve

70, 71, 72...79	80, 81, 82...89	90, 91, 92...99
setenta	ochenta	noventa
setenta y uno	ochenta y uno	noventa y uno
setenta y dos	ochenta y dos	noventa y dos
setenta y tres	ochenta y tres	noventa y tres
setenta y cuatro	ochenta y cuatro	noventa y cuatro
setenta y cinco	ochenta y cinco	noventa y cinco
setenta y seis	ochenta y seis	noventa y seis
setenta y siete	ochenta y siete	noventa y siete
setenta y ocho	ochenta y ocho	noventa y ocho
setenta y nueve	ochenta y nueve	noventa y nueve

100	cien, ciento
200	doscientos/as
300	trescientos/as
400	cuatrocientos/as
500	quinientos/as
600	seiscientos/as
700	setecientos/as
800	ochocientos/as
900	novecientos/as
1000	mil
10,000	diez mil
100,000	cien mil
1,000,000	un millón
1,000,000,000	mil millones
100,000,000,000	cien mil millones
1,000,000,000,000	un billón

Notes about numbers

There is a distinction between "uno" and "un/una" (see next, *Chapter 6 Masculine/Feminine*). "Uno" can only be used when it refers to a number, not a quantity of something.

twenty one; twenty one albums, twenty one hours
veintiuno; ventiún álbumes; ventiuna horas

The word "cien" changes to "ciento" when it is not one hundred even.

100 albums;   101 albums;   190 albums
cien álbumes; ciento un álbumes; ciento noventa álbumes

100,000 albums; 1,100 albums
cien mil álbumes; mil cien álbumes

The words doscientos (200), trescientos (300),... novecientos (900) change to doscientas, trescientas, ...novecientas if the word that follows is feminine (*Chapter 6 Masculine/Feminine*).

Five hundred people
Quinientas personas

The word "millón" in Spanish needs the word "de" (= of), unlike English.

100 hours; 1,000 hours; 1,000,000 hours
cien horas; mil horas;   un millón de horas

In Spanish figures are never expressed in terms of hundreds.

2100 = two thousand one hundred or twenty one hundred
2100 = dos mil cien (not veintiún cientos)

"Billón" in Spanish is not billion in English, but 1,000,000,000,000. "Mil millones" is one billion.

Telling the Time

To refer to a time or ask for the time:

> What's the time?
> ¿Qué hora es?
>
> **At** what time is the appointment?
> **¿A** qué hora es la cita?

As in English there are **two forms** to tell the time:

> It's one fifteen.   = It's a quarter past one.
> Es la una y quince. = Es la una y cuarto.

One Form	The Other Form	Time
Son las doce y 45	Es la una menos cuarto.	12:45
Es la una	Es la una en punto.	1:00
Es la una y 15.	Es la una y cuarto.	1:15
Es la una y 30.	Es la una y media.	1:30
Son las dos.	Son las dos en punto.	2:00
Son las dos y 5.		2:05
Son las dos y 10.		2:10
Son las dos y 15.	Son las dos y cuarto.	2:15
Son las dos y 20.		2:20
Son las dos y 25.		2:25
Son las dos y 30.	Son las dos y media.	2:30
Son las dos y 35.	Son las tres menos 25.	2:35
Son las dos y 40.	Son las tres menos 20.	2:40
Son las dos y 45.	Son las tres menos cuarto.	2:45
Son las dos y 50.	Son las tres menos 10.	2:50
Son las dos y 55.	Son las tres menos 5.	2:55

Telling the Date

In Spanish, when telling the date, the day always precedes the month.

What day of the week is today? Today is Saturday.
¿Qué día es hoy?   Hoy es Sábado.

What date is today? Today is February 21, 2007.
¿Qué día es hoy?   Hoy es (el) 21 de Febrero de 2007.

Month	Mes	Month	Mes
January	Enero	July	Julio
February	Febrero	August	Agosto
March	Marzo	September	Septiembre
April	Abril	October	Octubre
May	Mayo	November	Noviembre
June	Junio	December	Diciembre

Tips

Frequently Asked Questions

FAQ 1: What's the plural of words like "cactus?"

Like English, Spanish has a reduced number of words that have an irregular plural, like cactus.

un cactus, dos cactus, tres cactus
(= a cactus, two cacti, three cacti)

In general, Spanish words ending in "–us," "–is" don't change. An exception is gris-grises (= gray).

crisis - crisis, análisis - análisis, tesis -tesis
(= crisis - crises, analysis - analyses, thesis - theses)

Some words ending in "–í" can change to "íes," e.g. iraní, iranies (= Iranian, Iranians).

FAQ 2: Can I express years in hundreds?

No, in Spanish no quantity (not only years) is expressed in hundreds.

In nineteen forty (1940)...
En mil novecientos cuarenta... (not En diecinueve cuarenta)

Exercise

Spell out the following figures:

253   153   1,101   1,929   2,128   5,100

This exercise is for you to "say" the numbers; the spelling of the figures is not important (since you always use the symbols of the numbers).

Answers

253   doscientos cincuenta y tres
153   ciento cincuenta y tres
1,101   mil ciento uno
1,929   mil novecientos veintinueve
2,128   dos mil ciento veintiocho
5,100   cinco mil cien

General Vocabulary

Days of the week

English	Spanish
Monday	lunes *
Tuesday	martes
Wednesday	miércoles
Thursday	jueves
Friday	viernes
Saturday	sábado
Sunday	domingo

(*) In Spanish, the week starts on Monday, not on Sunday.

The translation of the "on" of "**on** Monday, on Tuesday" is "**el** lunes, **el** martes…"

Months of the year

English	Spanish
January	Enero
February	Febrero
March	Marzo
April	Abril
May	Mayo
June	Junio
July	Julio
August	Agosto
September	Septiembre
October	Octubre
November	Noviembre
December	Diciembre

The translation of "in" (in January) is "en" (en Enero).

The translation of "first" of January is "el uno" de Enero (literally: the one of Enero). Notice that Spanish doesn't use the ordinals (first, second, third…) for dates, as English does (e.g. first of June).

Time units (in natural order)

English	Spanish
year	año
month	(el) mes
week	semana
day	día
hour	hora
minute	minuto
second	segundo

Other words to express time

English	Spanish
and	y
date	fecha
half	media
is	es
minus	menos
of	de
quarter (1/4)	cuarto
now	ahora, ahorita
the	el/ la
today	hoy
Today is Tuesday	Hoy es Martes.
tomorrow	mañana
what	qué
What day is it today?	¿Qué día es hoy?
yesterday	ayer

Location

English	Spanish
here	aquí, acá
there	allí, allá, ahí

Underlined indicates the stress of the word

In parenthesis el/la indicates masculine/feminine, which normally end in "o" (if masculine) or "a" (if feminine)

Technical Vocabulary

Construction I

Layout

English	Spanish
construction	(la) construcción
layout, floor plan	planta, (el) *layout*
area	(el) área
attic, penthouse	ático
basement	sótano
corridor, landing	(el) corredor, pasillo
entry, vestibule	entrada, vestíbulo
floor, story	planta, piso
ground floor	bajo, planta baja
first floor	(el) primer piso
kitchen	cocina
lift shaft	hueco del ascensor
mezanine	(el) *mezanine*, entreplanta
open area	(el) área abierta
parking area	estacionamiento
porch	(el) porche
ramp	rampa
riser shaft	patinillo de instalaciones
roof	techo
room	cuarto, sala, pieza
living room, dining room	sala, cuarto de estar, (el) comedor
bedroom	dormitorio, recámara
bathroom	baño, cuarto de baño
restrooms	(los) aseos, (los) baños, (los) servicios
utility room	cuarto de servicio
stairs	escalera
terrace, balcon	terraza, (el) balcón
walk-in closet	(el) vestidor, (el) closet
yard, patio	patio
front yard	patio de delante
back yard	patio de atrás

Types of Constructions

English	Spanish
airport	aeropuerto
apartment, flat	apartamento, piso
aqueduct	acueducto
bridge	(el) puente
building	edificio
house	casa
apartment building	edificio de apartamentos
office building	edificio de oficinas
industrial building	(la) nave industrial
parking building	edificio de aparcamientos
dam	presa, represa
industry	industria
freeway, highway	autopista
factory	fábrica
lot	(el) área
parcel of land	parcela
park	(el) parque
parking lot	aparcamiento al aire libre
path	camino, sendero
port	puerto
power plant	(la) central, (la) central de energía
nuclear power plan	(la) central nuclear
road (car road)	carretera
single family dwelling	(el) chalet, casa
street	(la) calle
workshop	(el) taller

6. MASCULINE / FEMININE
MASCULINO / FEMENINO

Some nouns have gender. In both English and Spanish, there are words that reflect this.

boy/girl,	lion/lioness,	actor/actress
niño/niña,	león/leona,	actor/actriz

However English nouns referring to things generally don't have gender. There are exceptions (lion/lioness). Generally, English divides the world into living and non-living things. Gender applies only to living things (he, she, man, woman, etc.). Spanish categorizes all entities into masculine and feminine.

English makes no additional distinction whether the word is masculine or feminine. Spanish does. In Spanish all words around a noun (i.e. determiners and adjectives) must have the same gender as the noun.

<u>a</u> lion   / <u>a</u> lioness
<u>un</u> león/ <u>una</u> leona

<u>the</u> <u>small</u> boy   / <u>the</u> <u>small</u> girl
<u>el</u> niño <u>pequeño</u> / <u>la</u> niña <u>pequeña</u>

In addition, Spanish assigns a gender to **every noun**, i.e. every object, material or immaterial, can be masculine or feminine. Examples:

- Masculine: cemento, kilo, carro, sonido, yate
  (= cement, kilo, car, sound, yacht)

- Feminine: guitarra, isla, hora, avenida, luz
  (= guitar, island, hour, avenue, light)

However, the words around the noun (determiners and adjectives) don't have an **intrinsic** gender. The same word can change masculine and feminine. Example: americano (= American) is an adjective, and it can be americano (masculine) or americana (feminine).

niño americano (= American boy)
niña americana (= American girl)

Rules help students recognize if a noun is masculine or feminine. These rules are based on the endings of words (meaningful endings of words are called "suffixes").

Basic Rules to Know the Gender of a Word

Golden Rule

> Words ending in an "**o**" **tend** to be masculine; words ending in an "**a**" **tend** to be feminine.

For example: el cemento, la guitarra. There are exceptions, for instance: (el) mapa, (la) mano.

Other basic rules of gender are:

- Words ending in "**-ma**" tend to be masculine, e.g. el dilema (= dilemma), el problema (= problem). There are exceptions: la calma (= calm).

- Words ending in "**-dad**," and "**-ción**" are feminine, e.g. la identidad, la diversidad, la realidad, la solución, la intervención, la atracción (= identity, diversity, reality, solution, intervention, attraction). Notice that "-dad" and "-ción" correspond to the English "-ty" and "-tion."

- Words ending in "**-ista**" ("-ist" in English) will be masculine or feminine depending on the person who is

referred to, e.g. el artista (= artist) Pablo Picasso, la artista
Frida Kahlo.

Besides, certain groups of nouns have a defined gender:

- The names of the letters are feminine, e.g: la A, la Be, la Ce,
  etc.

- The names of the numbers are masculine: el uno, el dos, el
  tres, etc. (= one, two, three, etc.)

- The names of countries tend to be masculine unless ending
  in "a." e.g. Brasil (masculine), España (feminine); "Brasil
  es lindo, España es linda" (= Brazil is beautiful, Spain is
  beautiful").

- Foreign words tend to be masculine, unless ending in "a."
  e.g. el software; la pizza

Collections are masculine: When you have a collection of names, with
masculine **and** feminine elements in it, use the masculine gender.

I have four daughters and one son: they are my children.
Tengo cuatro hijas y un hijo: son mis hijos.

My uncles and aunts live in Texas.
Mis tíos viven en Texas.

Spain and Brazil are beautiful.
España y Brasil son lindos.

From now on, it's important that you memorize nouns with their proper
gender. In Spanish dictionaries, the first information that is presented
about a noun is whether it is masculine or feminine.

Warning

Here are some basic rules that will help you. However, there are many
exceptions. It is important when you learn a new word from the
dictionary, you learn it with its gender (Remember: only nouns have
gender).

General Vocabulary

Articles and demonstratives (in natural order)

English	Spanish
a	un, una
the	el, la, los, las
this	este/ a
this thing	esto
these...	estos/as
that	ese/ a
that thing	eso
those...	esos/ as
that...over there	aquel, aquella
that thing over there	aquello
those... over there	aquellos/as
to the, at the	al (a + el)
of the	del (de + el)

Possessives (in natural order)

English	Spanish
my	mi, mis
your (singular)	tu, tus
his (as in "his house")	su, sus
her	su, sus
its	su, sus
our	nuestro/a/os/as
your (you guys) (Spain)	vuestro/a/os/as
your (you guys)	su, sus (de ustedes)
their	su, sus

Other limiting adjectives

English	Spanish
a lot	mucho
a lot of...	mucho/ a/ os/ as
a lot of...	un montón de...
all...	todo/ a/ os/ as
another	otro/ a
any, whichever	cualquiera
any..., whichever	cualquier...
both	los dos
everything	todo
little (amount)	poco
little (amount)...	poco/ a ...
much	mucho / a
much	muchos/ as
no...	ningún, nunguna
none	ninguno / ninguna
none of...	ninguno/a de ...
nothing	nada
other, others	otro/ a/ os /as
some	alguno / a/ os/ as
some of ...	alguno / a/ os/ as de...
some...	algún / a/ os/ as
some...	unos, unas
something	algo

If you have started your vocabulary list, make sure that you write the right gender of every word on it.

In addition, the following lists are suggested to be included.

Technical Vocabulary

Construction II

Elevation

English	Spanish
elevation	**alzado**
beam	viga
arc	arco
lintel	(el) dintel
vault	bóveda
floor	suelo
baseboard, skirting board	(el) rodapié
carpet	moqueta, alfombrado
concrete slab	forjado
parquet floor	(el) parqué
plant	planta
raised floor	falso suelo
foundations	(los) cimientos
pillar	pilar
brickwork pillar	(el) machón, pilar de fábrica
column	columna
wood pilar	(el) pie derecho
roof	cubierta
crown molding	rodatecho
false ceiling	falso techo
skylight	lucernario
truss	cercha
wall	(la) pared, cerramiento
facade	fachada
load-bearing wall	muro de carga
parapet	peto
partition	(el) tabique
wall face	paramento
wood/glass partition	mampara

Miscellaneous

English	Spanish
construction	(la) construcción
construction site	obra
construction works	obra
coat	capa
drawing, blueprint	plano
layout, floor plan	planta, (el) *layout*
elevation	alzado
section drawing	sección
detail drawing	plano de detalle
sketch	(el) croquis, dibujo
demolition	(la) demolición
ditch	zanja
door	puerta
gate	puerta
earthworks	movimiento de tierras
expansion joint	junta de dilatación
fence	cerca, valla
finishing	acabado
frame	marco
furniture	mobiliario
diesel generator set	grupo electrógeno
gutter	canaleta
drainpipe	(la) bajante
handrail	barandilla
hole	agujero
hollow	Hueco, zanja
land	tierra
level	(el) nivel
load (structural load)	carga
torque	(el) par
pressure	(la) presión
force	fuerza
weight	peso
move	mudanza
openwork wall	muro palomero
plumb-bob, plummet	plomada
scaffold	andamio
scaffolding	(el) andamiaje

English	Spanish
sheet	plancha, chapa
step	(el) escalón
structure	estructura
trowel	llana
window	ventana
work shed	caseta de obra

7. CONJUGATION
CONJUGACIÓN

Verbs are the nuclei of the sentence. A sentence can lack nearly anything but a verb. Verbs are all those words that describe what the subject (the person or thing) does. Examples of verbs:

> to repeat, to posses, to declare, to prefer, to toast
> repetir, poseer, declarar, preferir, tostar

Let's see a verb in action with other elements:

> <u>He</u>   <u>cancelled</u>   <u>his</u>   <u>ticket.</u>
> NOUN   VERB   DET.   NOUN

Every verb has many possible forms: For example, the English verb "to sing" has the variations:

> sing, sings, sang, sung, singing

We change the form of the verb depending on who is doing the action (I sing, he sings, …), and depending on when the action occurs (I sing, I sang, I will sing…).

Conjugating a verb means to put the verb in its different forms. For example, in English, the **conjugation** of the verb "to be" in the present tense is:

I am
You are
He/ She/ It is
We are
You guys are
They are

If you looked up the words "studied," "studies" or "studying" in the English dictionary you may not find them. This is because all tenses of the verb "to study" are represented only by the word "study." The form of the verb with the preposition "to" (to study) is called **the infinitive**.

Golden Rule 1

> In Spanish, the infinitive (the proxy of the verb) **always** ends with -AR, -ER or –IR.

For example:

estudi**ar**, correspond**er**, distribu**ir**
(= to study, to correspond, to distribute)

Those three endings correspond to three patterns called "conjugaciones" (= conjugations).

It's important that you learn these names:

- Verbs ending in -AR are called **AR-verbs,** or verbs of the **first conjugation.**

- Verbs ending in -ER are called **ER-verbs**, or verbs of the **second conjugation**.

- Verbs ending in -IR are called **IR-verbs**, or verbs of the **third conjugation.**

Thus, for example, you probably won't find it in the dictionary the word "estudia" (= he studies); you must look for "estudi**ar**" (= to study) which is the infinitive, the representative of its family.

The dictionary will also tell you if the verb is regular or irregular, in other words, if the verb follows the rules when it is conjugated.

English puts the information of who makes the action (I, you, he/she/it, we, you, they) before the verb (I do something). On the contrary,

Spanish puts this information **within** the verb, at the end of the verb, as a suffix.

> We adore theatre. They paint houses.
> Adoramos el teatro. Pintan casas.

Before studying those endings (as the "n" in "pintan"), you must see the translation of the pronouns: I, you, etc.

Spanish	English
yo	= I
tú	= you singular, informal
usted	= you – singular, formal
él / ella / ello	= he/ she/ it
nosotros/ nosotras	= we
vosotros/ vosotras	= you plural, only in Spain
ustedes	= you plural
ellos /ellas	= they (masculine/ feminine)

Golden Rule 2

In Spanish the subject of the sentence is always **within** the verb The translations of the English personal pronouns are suffixes: particles at the end of the verb. These are:

English	Spanish	Example
I	−VOWEL [1] or −y	planeo, soy (= I plan, I am)
you (singular informal)	−s [2]	invitas (= you invite)
you (singular formal), he/she/it	−VOWEL [1]	cuenta (= he/she counts)
We	−mos	convencemos (= we convince)
you guys (Spain)	−is	aparecéis (= you appear)
you guys, They	−n [3]	estudian (= you/ they study)

(^{1}) These VOWELS can be: a, e, i, o, depending on the tense. For example: canto (= I sing), canté (= I sang)

(^{2}) This is the informal "you". As explained later in this book the ending "s" has three exceptions: the past and the imperative tenses, and the verb "ser" (= to be).

(^{3}) In Latin America the forms of "you guys" and "they" coincide. Thus, "aparecen" means "you guys appear" and also "they appear." The words "ustedes" (= you guys) and "ellos" (= they) are used to avoid ambiguity. See *Appendix A Notes about Dialects.*

The Personal Pronouns

Spanish does have personal pronouns such as: I, you, he, she, etc., but using them would be redundant because the information on who makes the action is already in the verb itself. So, we recommend <u>not</u> to use them unless necessary to avoid confusion.

English Pronoun	Spanish Pronoun	Spanish endings
I	yo	–VOWEL / –y
you (singular informal)	tú	–s
you (singular formal) → he/she →	usted él, ella	–VOWEL
We	nosotros	–mos
you guys (Spain)	vosotros	–is
you guys → They →	ustedes ellos	–n

Examples

yo	[yo] Estoy contento. (= I am content)
tú	[tú] Estás contento. (=You are content)
usted él, ella	[usted] Está contento. (= You are content.) [Él] Está contento. (= He is content.)
nosotros	[nosostros] Estamos contentos. (= We are content)
vosotros	[vosotros] Estáis contentos. (= You guys are content)
ustedes ellos	[ustedes] Están contentos. (= You guys are content) [ellos] Están contentos. (= They are content.)

The word in [ ] can be omitted in the sentence.

Warning: Notice that the forms of "usted" are the same as those of "él/ella". To avoid ambiguity, the words "usted" or "él/ella" are used. The same happens with the pronouns:"ustedes" and "ellos."

There is a word for "it", the pronoun "ello," but this pronoun is omitted. For example:

> It is raining.
> Está lloviendo.

The pronouns are only used to either answer "who?", to emphasize, or to avoid ambiguity.

> ¿Quién responde? **Nosotros.**
> Who responds? We do.

> **Ella** tiene que reescribir la carta; no tú.
> She has to re-write the letter; not you.

> ¿**Usted** está enfermo? ("Está enfermo" also means "él/ella)
> Are you sick?

Appendix A, Notes about Dialects, shows the use of the pronouns according to the three main dialects.

Regular Verbs

The remaining portion of the verb when we remove the AR/ER/IR part of its infinitive is called the stem. For example: the stems of:

> admirar, responder, describir

are:

> admir-, respond-, describ-

(as we saw in Golden Rule 1).

A verb is called regular when the corresponding endings for all persons (I, you, he, etc.) coincide with the regular endings

Let's see examples of the present tense of verbs of the three Spanish conjugations:

> admir**ar** (= to admire) is an **AR**-verb, also called a verb of the **first** conjugation.
> respond**er** (= to respond) is an **ER**-verb, also called a verb of the **second** conjugation.
> describ**ir** (= to describe) is an **IR**-verb, also called a verb of the **third** conjugation.

to admire	= admirar
I admire	admir**o**
You admire	admir**as**
He/She/It admires	admir**a**
We admire	admir**amos**
You guys admire (Spain)	admir**áis** (Spain)
You guys/ They admire	admir**an**

to respond	= responder
I respond	respond**o**
You respond	respond**es**
He/She/ It responds	respond**e**
We respond	respond**emos**
You guys respond	respond**éis** (Spain)
You guys/ They respond	respond**en**

to describe	= describir
I describe	describo
You describe	describes
He/She describes	describe
We describe	describimos
You guys describe	describís (Spain)
You guys / They describe	describen

The verbs "ser" and "estar" (= to be)

You will use "estar" as "to be" when the attribute is temporary, for example:

I am content.
Estoy contento.

But "to be" has another translation, "ser"." The verb "ser" is used when the attribute is permanent.

I am from Peru.
Soy de Perú.

The conjugation of these verbs are:

	ser	**estar**
(I)	soy	estoy
(you singular)	eres	estás
(he/she/it)	es	está
(we)	somos	estamos
(you guys)- Spain-	sois	estáis
(you guys/ they)	son	están

Warning

Certain expressions that use "to be" in English, use another verb in Spanish: "tener."

For example:

I am hungry/ thirsty/ hot/ cold/ sleepy/ twenty years old.
Tengo hambre/ sed/ calor/ frío/ sueño/ veinte años.

"Tener" (= to have)

"Tener" is equivalent to "to have got." So, it means to possess, or to grasp.

> I've got a house. = I posses a house.
> I've got a chair. = I grasp a chair.

It is important that you associate "tener" with "to have got", instead of simply "to have," which can be another verb in Spanish (haber). We will see in *Chapter 9 One Future, Present and Past.*

The expression "I have to" in Spanish also uses the verb "tener. "

> **I've got to** cancel the appointment.
> **Tengo que** cancelar la cita.

The conjugation of *tener* is:

	tener
(I)	tengo
(you singular)	tienes
(he/she/it)	tiene
(we)	tenemos
(you guys) -Spain-	tenéis
(you guys/ they)	tienen

Tips

Frequently Asked Question

FAQ: "Vosotros" or "ustedes" (= you plural)?

> "Vosotros" (= you guys) is only used in Spain. It uses the form of the second person of plural, e.g.

> vosotros cantáis (= you guys sing)

"Ustedes" means "you guys" (informal) in Latinoamerica and means "you, sirs" or "you, ma'ams"(formal) in Spain. Regardless of this, "ustedes" doesn't use the forms of the second person plural, but the forms of the third person of plural, e.g.

> ustedes cantan (= you guys sing) not ~~ustedes cantáis~~

In the same way, "usted " means "you singular (and formal) in Latinoamerica, and means "you, sir" or "you, ma'am"(formal) in Spain. Regardless of this, "usted" doesn't use the forms of the second person of singular, but the forms of the third person of singular, e.g.

> usted canta (= you -singular- sing)   not ~~usted cantas~~.

This book teaches the complete range of verb forms: the six persons (all the verb tables of this book have six rows). The forms of "vosotros," i.e. the forms of the second person plural, are exceptionally regular.

The use of "usted" and "ustedes" is also explained in *Appendix A, Notes About Dialects*.

General Vocabulary

Personal pronouns

English	Spanish
I	yo
you – singular, informal	tú
you – singular, formal	usted
he/ she/ it	él / ella / *
we	nosotros/ as
you – plural (Spain)	vosotros/ as
you – plural	ustedes
they	ellos /as

> (*) The word "it" as in "It is my house" is not
> translated in Spanish: "Es mi casa."

The verbs for "to be" (= ser/ estar)

The verb "to be" use two verbs: *ser* and *estar* in Spanish. *Ser* is used
for permanent attributes; *estar* for non-permanent attributes. Example:

> Martin **is** from the Unites States. Martin **is** in Italy now.
> Martín **es** de los Estados Unidos. Martin **está** en Italia ahora.

The following is the conjugation for the present tense of the verbs
"ser" and "estar."

English	Spanish	
to be	**ser**	**estar**
I am	soy	estoy
You (singular) are	eres	estás
He/ She/ It is	es	está
We are	somos	estamos
You guys are (Spain)	sois	estáis
You guys/ They are	son	están

Remember that the underscore mark is just a hint in this book to tell you where the stressed vowel is, and to make it easier to learn the words with their correct pronunciation.

The verbs for "to have" (= tener/ haber)

English	Spanish
to have	**tener**
I have	tengo
You have	tienes
He/ She/ It has	tiene
We have	tenemos
You guys have (Spain)	tenéis
You guys/ They have	tienen

Sample of descriptive adjectives that use "ser"

English	Spanish
American (from the US)	americano/ a
Cuban	cubano/ a
Dominican	dominicano/ a
Mexican	mejicano/ a, mexicano/ a
Puerto Rican	puertorriqueño/ a

Sample of descriptive adjectives that use "estar"

English	Spanish
alive	vivo
asleep	dormido
dead	muerto
healthy	sano
nervous	nervioso
sick	enfermo
tired	cansado
worried	preocupado
wounded	herido

Technical Vocabulary

Materials

Construction materials

English	Spanish
material	(el) material
ceramic product	cerámica
brick	ladrillo
roof tile	teja
floor tile	baldosa
cement block	(el) bloque de cemento
concrete block	(el) bloque de hormigón
cobblestone	(el) adoquín
stone	piedra
sheet rock	Pladur®, placa de yeso
aggregate	árido
sand	arena
gravel	grava
binder (*[1])	(el) conglomerante
clay	arcilla, barro
terracotta	terracota
mud	barro
adobe (*[2])	(el) adobe
plaster (material)	yeso
white plaster	escayola, yeso blanco
gypsum	(el) mineral de yeso
lime	(la) cal
quicklime	(la) cal viva
slaked lime	(la) cal apagada, cal muerta
limestone	roca caliza
calcite	calcita
cement	cemento
mortar	mortero
lime mortar	mortero de cal, argamasa
cement mortar	mortero de cemento
concrete	(el) hormigón, concreto
reinforced concrete	(el) hormigón armado

English	Spanish
work (as in brickwork)	fábrica
stonework	fábrica de piedra
blockwork	fábrica de bloques
carpentry	carpintería
wood carpentry	carpintería de madera
aluminum carpentry	carpintería de aluminio
rendering	revestimiento
cement render	enfoscado/ guarnecido (*[3])
plaster	revoco (*[4])
white gypsum-based plaster	enlucido, encalado

Notes

*[1] Binder, as plaster, lime or cement.
*[2] Adobe is sand, clay and water.
*[3] "Enfoscado" is cement render using any mortar. "Guarnecido" is cement render using black plaster.
*[4] "Revoco" can be gypsum-based or lime-based plaster.

Fluids

English	Spanish
fluid	fluido
air	(el) aire
alcohol	el) alcohol
carbon dioxide CO_2	CO_2 dióxido de carbono
carbon monoxide CO	CO monóxido de carbono
diesel fuel	gasóleo
gasoline	gasolina
glue	pegamento
hydrogen	hidrógeno
lubricant	(el) lubricante
natural gas	(el) gas natural
nitrogen	nitrógeno
oil	(el) aceite
oil (petroleum)	petróleo
oxygen	oxígeno
water	(el) agua
water vapor	(el) vapor de agua

Miscellaneous

English	Spanish
aluminum	aluminio
oxide	óxido
acid	ácido
base	(la) base
salt	(la) sal
alloy	(la) aleación
coal	(el) carbón
element	elemento
mineral	(el) mineral
rock	roca
compound	compuesto
esparto	esparto
fiberglass	f ibra de vidrio
formica	formica
foam	espuma
glass	vidrio
gel	(el) gel
ice	hielo
iron	hierro
mixture	mezcla
natural product	producto natural
chemical	producto químico
paste	pasta
paint	pintura
plastic	plástico
powder	polvo (it also means "dust")
PVC	(el) PVC (pe uve ce)
raw material	materia prima
solid	sólido
liquid	líquido
gas	(el) gas
steel	acero
wood	madera
sawdust	(el) serrín

8. HOW TO LEARN WORDS EFFICIENTLY
CÓMO APRENDER PALABRAS EFICIENTEMENTE

As we saw in the last three chapters, when you look up a word in the dictionary, you must look for the proxy of that word. Examples:

> "carro" (singular), not "carros" (plural)
> "gato" (masculine), not "gata" (feminine)
> "estudiar" (infinitive), not "estudié" (= to study, not studied)

The proxy must be singular and masculine (if the word is a noun, determiner or adjective) and infinitive (if the word is a verb).

As for the meaning, we can classify words in two main categories:

> **Non-grammatical words** are those words with an actual meaning by itself: dog, white, walking, Peter, fast, attitude,…These are the words that you can describe when you play the party game charades.

> **Grammatical words** are those words that create the structure of the sentence: the, a, at, to, over, however, maybe, on, another, by...

You could only communicate very primitively without grammatical words. Grammatical words form the structure of the sentence. For example, in the sentence "Your cat is on the table," if you removed the grammatical words the result would be absurd:

> (Your) cat is (on the) table → cat is table

Regarding the non-grammatical words: you will have to choose which of these words you want to learn every day according to your areas of specialty: emergency, cardiology, etc. There's a reason for this: The words that you pick yourself will be the ones that you will enjoy memorizing, and the ones that you will end up utilizing. This book will give you recommendations and clues to look up non-grammatical words in the dictionary.

Regarding the grammatical words, *Chapter 11 Grammar Rules*, will go over these words extensively. Some will be explained in the body of each chapter, others will appear in the vocabulary section of each chapter.

We recommend the following method. Take it as a **golden rule.**

> - **Learn a consistent number of words a day** (say ten). Flash cards are a great idea to test yourself; in turn, using a computer spreadsheet for those words is the best way to keep a record. It enables you to sort your learned words and keep them organized.
>
> - **Pick your own words**. Select the grammatical words from this book, and the non-grammatical words from your areas of interest. Lists or families of words work better than unlinked words. For example, if you are keen on painting, learn the list of basic colors as part of your daily set of words (vs., one color and nine other words today, and another color with another nine words tomorrow).
>
> - **Notice if the words you are picking have similarities with English in any form**. Being aware of the commonalities will help you not only memorize the word but also memorize other words of its family.

Cognates, Indirect Cognates and False Cognates

A distinction can be made regarding the similar words in both languages. On one hand, there are "**cognates**," those words from Spanish that are easy to translate and recognize, for instance teléfono/telephone or artista/artist.

On the other hand, there is what we can call "**indirect cognates**," those words whose similarities are not evident, but are based on other words of the same family. For instance, "agua" is not a cognate of "water;" however, you can find the meaning through the cognate: aquarium/acuario.

There are hundreds of cognates, and hundreds of indirect cognates. Below you will find a list of indirect cognates:

English	Spanish	Cognate English/Spanish
big	grande	grand = gran
body	cuerpo	corporal = corporal
brain	cerebro	cerebral = cerebral
eye	ojo	ocular = ocular
field	campo	campus = campus
hand	mano	manual = manual
hundred	cien	cent = céntimo
ladder	escalera	escalator = escalera mecánica
lead	plomo	plumber = plomero
lung	pulmón	pulmonary = pulmonar
month	mes	semester = semestre
moon	luna	lunar = lunar
one	uno	unit = unidad
plane	avión	aviation = aviación
powder	polvo	to pulverize = pulverizar
sea	mar	submarine= submarino
skin	piel	to peel = pelar
stone	piedra	to petrificate = petrificar
sun	sol	solar = solar
thousand	mil	mile = milla
to see	ver	visible = visible
to sell	vender	vendor = vendedor
to sleep	dormir	dormant = durmiente
tooth	diente	dentist = dentista
tree	árbol	arboretum = arboreto
vessel	nave	navigate = navegar
water	agua	aquarium = acuario
year	año	annual = anual

A **false cognate** is a word that resembles another in the another language but has a different meaning. For example "constipated" sounds like "constipado," but the latter means "sick with a cold." Examples:

English	Spanish
constipated	estreñido
sick with a cold	constipado

English	Spanish
preservative	conservante
condom	preservativo, condón

English	Spanish
actual	real
current, today's	actual

Spanglish

Spanglish is what results when you insert English words (genuine or altered) in a Spanish speech or viceversa.

> Si tomo la **freeway**, llego allí antes.

This means: "If I take the freeway, I get there sooner;" where "freeway" is not a Spanish word.

In some cases, as the one above, the word is genuine: it has been taken from English as is (in spelling and pronunciation): La freeway, el bill, los taxes, el VCR, el U-turn, el e-mail, or el zip code. Other times, the word is altered: it has suffered some adaptation to the Spanish pronunciation:

> la troca (= truck), la marketa (= market), la yarda (= yard), las utilidades (= utilities), las partes (= auto-parts), lonchear (= to have lunch), parkear (= to park), likear (= to leak)

Occasionally, the newborn word can conflict with another word existing in the Spanish standard:

Non-standard Spanish	Standard Spanish
carpeta (= carpet)	carpeta (= folder)
remover (= to remove)	remover (= to stir)
ordenar (= to order food)	ordenar (= to command)

Prefixes and Suffixes

A prefix is an initial particle of a word with meaning. It is called suffix if it goes at the end of the word. For example the prefix "un" means "opposite." Thus, for example: "unnecessary" means "not necessary."

The vast majority of prefixes and suffixes are the same or very similar in both Spanish and English. Below, you will find just a sample:

English		Spanish	
-an	e.g. urban	-ano	e.g. urbano
-ic	e.g. atomic	-ico	e.g. atómico
-ism	e.g. urbanism	-ismo	e.g. urbanismo
-ist	e.g. specialist	-ista	e.g. specialista
-tion	e.g. preparation	-ción	e.g. preparación
-ty	e.g. integrity	-dad	e.g. integridad
anti-	e.g. anticorrosive	anti-	e.g. anticorrosivo
extra-	e.g. extraordinary	ex-	e.g. extraordinario
in-	e.g. to include	in-	e.g. incluir
post-	e.g. postgraduate	post-	e.g. postgraduado
pre-	e.g. prefabricated	pre-	e.g. prefabricado
re-	e.g. to repaint	re-	e.g. repintar
un-	e.g. unnecessary	in-	e.g. innecesario

Tips

Frequently Asked Question

FAQ: Where do I find the "grammatical words" that I have to learn?

> In the General Vocabulary at the end of each chapter, you will find relevant grammatical words related to the chapter. These words are included also in the *Index of Grammatical Words* at the end of the book.

General Vocabulary

Remember "tener" (to have got)
(seen in *Chapter 7 Conjugation*).

English	Spanish
to have got	tener
I have got	tengo
you (singular) have got	tienes
he/she/it has got	tiene
we have got	tenemos
you guys have got -Spain-	tenéis
you guys/ they have got	tienen

The verb "hacer" (= to make)

English	Spanish
to make	hacer
I make	hago
you (singular) make	haces
he/she/it makes	hace
we make	hacemos
you guys make- Spain-	hacéis
you guys/ they make	hacen

Nouns that go with "tener" (= to have got)
unlike English, which go with "to be" (= ser/ estar)

English	Spanish
hunger (e.g. I am hungry.)	(el) hambre (e.g. tengo hambre.)
thirsty	(la) sed
sleepy	sueño
60 years old	60 años
hot	(el) calor
cold	frío
scared	miedo

Nouns that go with "hacer" (= to make)

Unlike English, which go with "to be" (= ser/ estar)

English	Spanish
wind (e.g. It's windy)	viento (e.g. Hace viento *)
sunny	(el) sol
good wheather	buen tiempo
bad wheather	mal tiempo
cold	frío **
hot	(el) calor

(*) Notice that "hace" literally means "it makes" according to the table of the verb "hacer."

(**) Also notice that "hacer" will be used when the sentence is impersonal, e.g. "**Hace** frío" (= It's cold); unlike tener, which is used when the sentence is personal, e.g. "**Tengo** frío" (I am cold).

Spanglish

Some Spanish words are **only** found in the US. They are adaptations of Latin root words in the English language. They do not belong to the standard Spanish; however, they are very common in the U.S.

Some of the most popular ones are:

English	Spanglish	Spanish
application	(la) aplicación	(la) solicitud
form	forma	formulario
carpet	carpeta	alfombra
truck	troca	camioneta
eligibility	elegibilidad	(los) derechos
rent	renta	(el) alquiler
backyard	yarda	patio
utilities	utilidades	servicios de gas, etc.
auto-part	(la) parte	pieza

Technical Vocabulary

Electricity

Quantities

English	Spanish
quantity	(la) magnitud
capacitance	(la) capacidad
conductance	(la) conductancia
conductivity	conductividad
current intensity	(la) corriente, (la) intensidad
energy	(la) energía
impedance	impedancia
admittance	admitancia
inductance, coil	inductancia, bobina
magnetic field B	campo magnético B, (la) inducción mag.
magnetic field H	campo magnético H, excitación mag.
magnetic flux	flujo (magnético)
magnetic reluctance	(la) reluctancia (magnética)
power	potencia
real power	potencia activa
reactive power	potencia reactiva
aparent power	potencia aparente
power factor, cos φ	(el) factor de potencia, coseno de φ (fi)
resistance	resistencia
resistivity	(la) resistividad
voltage, tension	(el) voltaje, (la) tensión

Devices

English	Spanish
device	dispositivo
battery	batería
cable	(el) cable
cable tray	bandeja
main	acometida
line, wire	línea, hilo
phase	(la) fase
neutral	neutro

English	Spanish
earth, ground	tierra
earthing electrode	electrodo, pica de tierra
component	(el) componente
capacitor	(el) condensador
inductor	bovina, (el) inductor
resistor	resistencia
impedance	impedancia
power supply	(la) fuente de alimentación
electrode	electrodo
anode	ánodo
cathode	cátodo
electrical panel	cuadro eléctrico
generator	(el) generador
insulator	aislamiento, (el) aislante
junction box	caja de derivación
light bulb	bombilla, foco
light fixture	luminaria
lightning rod	(el) parrayos

Measuring Instruments

English	Spanish
measuring instrument	aparato de medida
ammeter	amperímetro
meter	(el) contador, (el) medidor
multimeter	multímetro
oscilloscope	osciloscopio
potentiometer	potenciómetro
voltmeter	voltímetro
wattmeter	vatímetro
motor	(el) motor
outlet	(el) enchufe
plug	(el) enchufe (macho), clavija
socket	(el) enchufe (hembra), toma de corriente
rectifier	(el) rectificador
switch	(el) interruptor
circuit breaker (c.b.)	(el) (interruptor) magnetotérmico
residual-current c.b.	(el) (interruptor) diferencial

English	Spanish
substation	(la) subestación
transformer	(el) transformador
UPS	*UPS* (u-pe-ese), SAI (sai)

UPS (uninterruptible power supply)
SAI= sistema de alimentacion initerrumpida

Concepts

English	Spanish
concept	concepto
AC	(la) corriente alterna
DC	(la) corriente continua
consumption	consumo
demand	demanda
electric charge	carga eléctrica
electricity	(la) electricidad
circuit	circuito
short circuit	cortocircuito
open circuit	circuito abierto
power circuit	circuito de fuerza
lighting circuit	circuito de alumbrado
electric field	campo eléctrico
harmonic	armónico
laser	(el) láser
lighting	(la) iluminación
load (power)	carga (eléctrica)
loss	pérdida
magnetic field	campo magnético
overload	sobrecarga
shunt	(el) *shunt*, (la) derivación
supply	suministro
Thevenin equivalent	(el) equivalente Thévenin
voltage drop	caída de tensión

SECTION III

SENTENCES
ORACIONES

Remember, from today on, it is recommended that you learn a number of words a day. Your daily set of words should be divided into two categories. One category is grammatical words. You will find many of them at the end of every chapter (General Vocabulary). For the other category, the non-grammatical words, you can pick them on your own depending on your areas of interest. Learn these words in groups.

Verbs are the essential part of sentences (you can't have a sentence without a verb). In the chapters 9 and 10, you will learn more about verbs.

You will learn about the different types of words (nouns, adjectives, verbs, etc.) in *Chapter 11 Grammar Rules.*

In the last chapter of this section, you will learn how to convert statements into questions and negative sentences.

When you finish Section III, you will be able to build your own sentences.

9. ONE FUTURE, PRESENT, AND PAST
UN FUTURO, PRESENTE Y PASADO

To start building sentences in the present, past, and future, we can use the three simplest Verb Structures: "I am singing, I am going to sing, I have sung." They are the simplest because there are few or no irregular verbs in these forms. The examples of this book use these three structures extensively.

These are the constructions to study:

> I am going to sing [future]   "Voy a cant**ar**"
> I am singing [present]   "Estoy cant**ando**"
> I have sung   [past]   "He cant**ado**"

Where:

> The form "to sing" is called the "infinitive" of the verb "to sing"
> The form "sing" is called the "gerund" of the verb "to sing"
> The form "sung" is called the "participle" of the verb "to sing"

Every conjugation (AR, ER, IR) has its own set of **endings**. In bold we have marked the endings that correspond to verbs for the three conjugations.

AR Verbs	ER Verbs	IR Verbs
-ar e.g cantar (= to sing)	**-er** e.g beber (= to drink)	**-ir** e.g vivir (= to live)
-ando e.g. cantando (= singing)	**-iendo** e.g bebiendo (= drinking)	**-iendo** e.g viviendo (= living)
-ado e.g. cantado (= sung)	**-ido** e.g bebido (= drunk)	**-ido** e.g vivido (= lived)

These three tenses (I am going to sing, I'm singing, , and I have sung) use three auxiliary verbs, which are: to be (estar), to go (ir) and to have (haber). In order to use these tenses appropriately you need to know the present tense of those three verbs.

One Future: "I am going to sing"

The structure "I am going to sing" uses the verb "ir" (=to go) conjugated, in other words, the verb "ir" changes with the persons I, you, he, etc.

Ir = to go

English	Spanish
I go	voy
you singular go	vas
he/she/it goes	va
we go	vamos
you guys go	vais (Spain)
you guys/ they go	van

Thus, I am going to sing, you are going to sing, etc. will be:

English		Spanish	
I am going	to sing	Voy	a cantar
You are going	to sing	Vas	a cantar
He/she is going	to sing	Va	a cantar
We are going	to sing	Vamos a cantar	
You guys are going	to sing	Vais	a cantar (Spain)
You guys/They are going	to sing	Van	a cantar

> Notice that the translation doesn't occur word for word: "*Voy a cantar*" is literally "I go to sing," but the translation is "I am going to sing."

> Other examples:

> I am going to establish a record.
> Voy a establecer un récord.

> They are going to divide the property.
> Van a dividir la propiedad.

One Present "I am singing"

The structure "I am singing" uses the verb "estar" (= to be) conjugated, in other words, the verb "estar" changes with the persons I, you, he, etc.

Estar = to be

English	Spanish
I am	estoy
You singular are	estás
He/she/it is	está
We are	estamos
You guys are (Spain)	estáis
You guys are/ they are	están

Thus, I am singing, You are singing, etc. will be:

English		Spanish	
I am	singing	Estoy	cantando
You are	singing	Estás	cantando
He is /she is	singing	Está	cantando
We are	singing	Estamos	cantando
You guys are	singing	Estáis	cantando (Spain)
You guys/ They are	singing	Están	cantando

> Unlike the structure we had before ("I am going to sing"), this is a literal translation: I am = *estoy*; singing = *cantando.*

> Other examples:

>> I am establishing a record.
>> Estoy estable**ciendo** un récord.

>> They are dividing the property.
>> Están divid**iendo** la propiedad.

One Past "I have sung"

The structure "I have sung" uses the verb "haber" (= to be) conjugated, in other words, the verb "haber" changes with the persons I, you, he, etc.

Haber = to have (auxiliary)

English	Spanish
I have (e.g. I have studied.)	he (e.g. He estudiado.)
You singular have	has
He/she/it has	ha
We have	hemos
You guys have (Spain)	habéis
You guys / They have	han

Thus, "I have sung," "you have sung," etc. will be:

English		Spanish	
I have	sung	He	cantado
You have	sung	Has	cantado
He/she has	sung	Ha	cantado
We have	sung	Hemos	cantado
You guys have	sung	Habéis	cantado (Spain)
You guys/ They have	sung	Han	cantado

This structure is a literal translation: I have = *he*; sung = *cantado*.

Other examples:

I have established a record.
He estable**cido** un récord.

They have divided the property.
Han divid**ido** la propiedad

Tips

Frequently Asked Questions

FAQ 1: Are there any verbs that don't follow the rules to construct the present, the past, or the future?

Few. In fact, the great advantages of learning these three tenses are the ease to memorize and the low number of irregular verbs in these tenses.

For example the verb "poner" (= to put) is irregular in the past tense. Thus, we write "puesto" instead of ~~ponido.~~

I have put the termometer there.
He puesto el termómetro allí.

This will be the topic of next chapter, *Chapter 10 Irregularities in the Future, Present and Past.*

FAQ 2: In English the forms "to sing", "singing," and "sung" can function as something different than a verb (an action). Is it the same in Spanish?

Yes, it is. Let's see this with some examples on the verb to drink and its forms drinking and drunk.

> **Drinking** is a problem.
> (Here the verb is "is" –to be. "Singing" functions as a noun. What is my passion? Singing).
>
> You won't solve your problems by **drinking** .
> (Here the verb is "to solve." "Drinking" functions as an adverb. **How** you won't solve your problems? Drinking).
>
> He is **drunk**.
> (Here the verb is "is" –to be. "drunk functions as an adjective. What is his attribute or condition? drunk).

Spanish is the same, with the exception of the first case. In the first case, Spanish uses the infinitive ("to drink", instead of "drinking").

> Beber es un problema.
> He esperado bebiendo.
> Está bebido.

Other examples:

> Acting in front of a large audience is my dream.
> Actuar en frente de una gran audiencia es mi sueño.
>
> I'm educating my voice by singing in the shower.
> Estoy educando mi voz cantando en la ducha.
>
> Are not you guys altering the document by eliminating the appendices?
> ¿No están (estáis –Spain-) alterando el documento al eliminar los apéndices?

General Vocabulary

The verb "ir" (= to go)

English	Spanish
to go	ir
I go	voy
you (singular) go	vas
he/she/it goes	va
we go	vamos
you guys go -Spain-	vais
you guys/ they go	van

Remember "estar," (= to be -temporal, *Chapter 7 Conjugation*)

English	Spanish
to be	estar
I am	estoy
You (singular) are	estás
He/ She/ It is	está
We are	estamos
You guys are -Spain-	estáis
You guys/ They are	están

The verb "haber" (= to have, as an auxiliary verb)

English	Spanish
to have (auxiliary)	haber
I have (e.g. I have studied.)	he (e.g. He estudiado.)
you (singular) have	has
he/she/it has	ha
we have	hemos
you guys have -Spain-	habéis
you guys/ they have	han

The only grammatical words among the verbs are the auxiliary verbs: to have (haber), to be (ser and estar), and to go (ir). When they act as auxiliary verbs they are a structural part of a sentence.

Technical Vocabulary

Electronics

Devices

English	Spanish
device	**dispositivo**
actuator	(el) actuador
antenna	antena
breadboard	placa de pruebas
CPU (*[1])	(el) CPU (ce-pe-u)
controller	(el) regulador
PID controller (*[2])	(el) regulador PID (pe-i-de)
diode	diodo
detector	(el) detector
gate, logic gate	puerta lógica
AND gate	puerta AND
inverter	(el) inversor
LED (light emitting diode)	(el) LED (led)
logic family	familia lógica
TTL (*[3])	(el) TTL (te-te-ele)
CMOS (*[4])	(el) CMOS (ce-mos)
microchip, integrated circuit	(el) chip, circuito integrado
chip socket	zócalo
package	cápsula
microcontroller	(el) microcontrolador
microprocessor	(el) microprocesador
operational amplifier	(el) amplificador operacional
photodiode	fotodiodo
pin	(el) pin, patilla
robot	(el) robot
satellite	(el) satélite
sensor	(el) sensor
terminal	(el) terminal
anode	ánodo
catode	cátodo
emitter	(el) emisor
base	(la) base

English	Spanish
collector	(el) colector
drain	(el) drenador
source	(la) fuente
thermistor	(el) termistor
thermocouple	(el) termopar
transducer	(el) trasductor
transistor	(el) transistor
npn BJT (*[5])	(el) transistor NPN (ene-pe-ene)
pnp BJT	(el) transistor PNP (pe-ene-pe)
p MOSFET (*[6])	(el) MOSFET (mos-fet) de canal p
n MOSFET	(el) MOSFET (mos-fet) de canal n
tyristor	(el) tiristor

Notes:

(*[1]) CPU, Central Processing Unit
(*[2]) PID, Proportional, integral, derivative
(*[3]) TTL, Transistor–transistor logic
(*[4]) CMOS, complementary metal-oxide-semiconductor
(*[5]) BJT, bipolar junction transistor
(*[6]) MOSFET, metal–oxide–semiconductor field-effect transistor

Concepts

English	Spanish
concept	**concepto**
bandwidth	ancho de banda
bit	(el) bit
control	(el) control
electron	(el) electrón
hole	hueco
Electronics	Electrónica
feedback	(el) realimentación
finite-state machine	máquina de estado
foton	(el) fotón

English	Spanish
Laplace transform	transform**a**da de *Laplace*
S transform	transform**a**da en s (**e**se)
Z transform	transform**a**da en z (zeta)
loop	(el) b**u**cle
PN junction	(la) unión PN (pe-**e**ne)
port	pu**e**rto
semiconductor	(el) semiconduct**o**r
signal	(la) señ**a**l
reset signal	(la) señ**a**l de r**e**set
clock signal	(la) señ**a**l de rel**o**j
transient event	(el) régimen transit**o**rio
steady state	(el) régimen perman**e**nte
truth table	t**a**bla de verd**a**d

10. IRREGULARITIES IN FUTURE, PRESENT, AND PAST
IRREGULARIDADES EN EL FUTURO, PRESENTE Y PASADO

Let's remember the endings:

AR Verbs	ER Verbs	IR Verbs
-ar e.g cantar (= to sing)	**-er** e.g beber (= to drink)	**-ir** e.g vivir (= to live)
-ando e.g. cantando (= singing)	**-iendo** e.g bebiendo (= drinking)	**-iendo** e.g viviendo (= living)
-ado e.g. cantado (= sung)	**-ido** e.g bebido (= drunk)	**-ido** e.g vivido (= lived)

Also remember:

> The form in AR, ER, IR is called **infinitive**.
> The form in ANDO, IENDO is called **gerund**.
> The form in ADO, IDO is called **participle** (or past participle)

A verb is irregular in the infinitive, gerund or participle (in other words: future, present or past) if it doesn't have the exact ending corresponding to future, present and past.

Thus, for example, the verb "morir" (= to die) is irregular in both the gerund and participle form, which are: "muriendo" and "muerto." By checking the table before, you see that the verb doesn't follow the rule:

IR verbs	if regular, it would be:	instead, it is:
-ir		morir (= to die)
-iendo	mor iendo	muriendo (= dying)
-ido	mor ido	muerto (= died)

Irregular Verbs in the Infinitive (to sing)

Let's remember the golden rule of *Chapter 7 Conjugation*:

> **All** verbs have their infinitive ending in AR, ER or IR. (The stem of the verb is what is left when you take out the ending AR, ER, or IR from its infinitive).

Thus, there is no irregular verb in the infinitive form.

Irregular Verbs in the Gerund (singing)

An example of an irregular verb in the gerund is "atribuir" (= to attribute). Its gerund is not ~~atribuiendo,~~ but atribuyendo.

There are four types of irregularities:

Type 1. Affects all verbs ending with -aer, -eer, -oer, -oír, -uir. e.g. atribuir.

These verbs insert a "y" between the stem and the ending, (otherwise it would sound strange with three vowels together)
e.g. atribu-ir → atribuiendo → atribuyendo (= attributing).

Infinitive		Gerund
atribuir	= to attribute	atribuyendo
caer	= to fall	cayendo
construir	= to construct	construyendo
contribuir	= to contribute	contribuyendo
creer	= to believe	creyendo
destruir	= to destruct	destruyendo
distribuir	= to distribute	distribuyendo
huir	= to flee	huyendo
incluir	= to include	incluyendo
leer	= to reed	leyendo
oír	= to hear	oyendo
poseer	= to posses	poseyendo
proveer	= to supply	proveyendo
traer	= to bring	trayendo

Type 2. Affects two verbs. Those IR verbs whose infinitive have an –o– in the second to last syllable.

These verbs change o → u, in order to form the gerund.

dor-mir → durmiendo   (= sleeping)

Infinitive		Gerund
dormir	= to sleep	durmiendo
morir	= to die	muriendo

Type 3. Affects all verbs of the third conjugation (IR verbs) whose infinitive have an -e- in the second to last syllable.

These verbs change e → i to form their gerund.

a-rre-pen-tir → arrepintiendo   (= repenting)

Examples:

Infinitive		Gerund
arrepentir	= to repent	arrepintiendo
conseguir	= to achieve	consiguiendo
convertir	= to convert	convirtiendo
corregir	= to correct	corrigiendo
decir	= to say	diciendo
despedir	= to see so. off./ to fire	despidiendo
divertir	= to have fun	divirtiendo
elegir	= to choose	eligiendo
freír	= to fry	friendo
gemir	= to wine	gimiendo
herir	= to cause a wound	hiriendo
hervir	= to boil	hirviendo
inferir	= to infer	infiriendo
invertir	= to invert	invirtiendo
medir	= to measure	midiendo
mentir	= to lie	mintiendo
pedir	= to ask for	pidiendo
preferir	= to prefer	prefiriendo
reír	= to laugh	riendo
rendir	= to surrender	rindiendo
reñir	= to quarrel	riñiendo
repetir	= to repeat	repitiendo
seguir	= to go on	siguiendo
sentir	= to feel	sintiendo
servir	= to serve	sirviendo
sonreír	= to smile	sonriendo
sugerir	= to suggest	sugiriendo
venir	= to come	viniendo
vestir	= to dress	vistiendo

You will also see similar irregularities in the present tense (*Chapter 16 The Present and Past Tenses*).

Type 4. Others.

There are only two verbs that don't conform to any rule for their irregularity. These are:

Infinitive		Gerund
ir	= to go	yendo
poder	= can	pudiendo

Irregular Verbs in the Past Participle (Sung)

There are only 13 common verbs with an irregular participle. For example, for "abrir" (= to open), it is "abierto," not abrido.

Below you'll find the list of verbs that are irregular in the Past Participle.

Infinitive		Past Participle
abrir	= to open	abierto
cubrir	= to cover	cubierto
escribir	= to write	escrito
decir	= to say	dicho
hacer	= to do	hecho
morir	= to die	muerto
poner	= to put	puesto
resolver	= to resolve	resuelto
romper	= to break	roto
satisfacer	= to satisfy	satisfecho
soltar	= to loosen up	suelto
volver	= to come back	vuelto
ver	= to see	visto

Tips

Frequently Asked Questions

FAQ: Are "died" and "dead" the same word in Spanish?

> Yes, they are: "muerto." Consider the English word "tired." It's the same for: "I am **tired**", and "I have **tired** him by running."

General Vocabulary

There are two types of words whose function is to join: the prepositions, which links parts of the sentence, and the conjunction, which joins one clause with another.

Preposiones

English	Spanish
about	sobre
according to	según
after	tras (*Voy tras él. = I go after him.*)
against	contra
around	alrededor de
at	a, en (*)
at, in, on	en, sobre (*)
at/ in the beginning of...	al principio de
at/ in the end of...	al final de
between, among	entre
by	para, por (*)
far from	lejos de
for	para, por (*)
in the middle of...	en medio de
inside...	dentro de
near, close to, around...	cerca de
next to...	junto a
of, from, off	de, desde (*)
on top of...	encima de
outside...	fuera de
side by side...	al lado de
to	para, a (*)
to, towards	hacia
under	bajo (*Está bajo la cama = It's under the bed*)
underneath	debajo de / abajo de (same as above)
until, up to	hasta
with	con
without	sin

(*) Translation varies depending on the context

Conjunctions

English	Spanish
although	aunque
and	y
as	a medida que
as	como
as per	en cuanto a…
as soon as	tan pronto como
because	porque
because of	por
because of	por causa de
but	pero
but	sino
due to	debido a
either…or…	o…o..
given that	dado que
however	sin embargo
if	si
I mean	o sea
in case that	en el caso de que
in other words	en otras palabras
in spite of	a pesar de
in view that	en vista de que/ visto que
like	al igual que
like	como
neither …nor…	ni…ni…
nevertheless	no obstante
or	o
since	puesto que/ ya que
so that	para que
then, afterwards	entonces
then, afterwards	luego
under the condition that	a condición de que
unless	a menos que
unlike	a diferencia de
while, as long as	mientras

Technical Vocabulary

Hardware and Software

Hardware

English	Spanish
hardware	(el) *hardware*
CD player	(el) reproductor de CDs
camera	cámara
video camera	cámara de vídeo
card	tarjeta
memory card	tarjeta de memoria
sound card	tarjeta de sonido
video card	tarjeta de vídeo
cell phone	(el) celular, (el) móvil
computer	(el) ordenador, (el/la) computador/a
DVD	(el) DVD (de-be-de)
disk	disco
fax	(el) fax
flash drive, pen drive	(el) lápiz de memoria
hard disk	disco duro
headphones	(los) auriculares
keyboard	teclado
laptop	(el) portátil
microphone	micrófono
modem	(el) módem
monitor	(el) monitor
mouse	(el) ratón
phone	teléfono
printer	impresora
scanner	(el) escáner
server	(el) servidor
speaker	(el) altavoz
tablet, ipad	tableta, (el) *ipad*

Software

English	Spanish
software	(el) *software*
application	(la) aplicación
at sign (@)	arroba
backup	copia de seguridad
CAD	CAD (cad)
configuration	(la) configuración
content	contenido
database	(la) base de datos
datum, data	dato, (los) datos
driver	(el) *driver*
email	(el) *email*, correo electrónico
encryptation	(la) encriptación
facebook	(el) *facebook*
graphic	gráfico
language	(el) lenguaje
C language	C (ce)
Java	*Java*
C++	C++ (ce más más)
list	lista
memory	memoria
menu	(el) menú
network	(la) red
page	página
program	(el) programa
protocole	(el) protocolo
spreadsheet	hoja de cálculo
symbol	símbolo
table	tabla
cell	celda
row	fila
column	columna
twit, twiter	(el) *twit*, (el) *twiter*
virus	(el) virus
web, WWW	(la) web
website	sitio web, página web
window	ventana
word processor	(el) procesador de textos

11. GRAMMAR RULES
REGLAS GRAMATICALES

Words can be divided into many ways but for the purpose of learning
effectively (fast), two main classifications arise. On one hand, words can
be classified into nine types according to their functionality in a sentence
(nouns, adjectives, verbs, etc.). On the other hand, overlapping this
classification, words can also be classified into two main groups
(grammatical and non grammatical words), depending on their having
either a structural value or a concrete meaning.

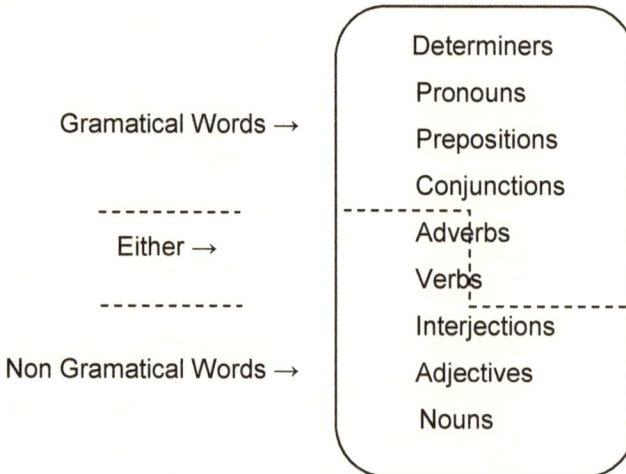

Gramatical Words →

- - - - - - - - - - -

Either →

- - - - - - - - - - -

Non Gramatical Words →

Determiners

Pronouns

Prepositions

Conjunctions

Adverbs

Verbs

Interjections

Adjectives

Nouns

The grammatical words are those words that you need to build a
sentence but that don't have a concrete meaning, for example:

in, or, other, not, my
en, o, otro,   no, mi

Conversely, **the non grammatical words** are those for which you can come out with a definition easily, for example:

> car,   gray, studying, rapidly
> carro, gris, estudiando, rápidamente

The importance of learning this categorization is to help you in the learning process and distinguish those words that have a structural importance (grammatical) from those that are "just vocabulary" (non grammatical). This book includes the *Index of Grammatical Words* for easy consultation at the end of the book.

As per the other classification, words can be:

- **Interjections** (interjecciones): Hello! Bye!
- **Determiners** (determinantes): the, a, an, five, these...
- **Adjectives** (adjetivos): green, large, true, productive...
- **Nouns** (nombres): Peter, house, truth, productivity...
- **Pronouns** (pronombres): we, us, ours, ourselves, me...
- **Adverbs** (adverbios) rapidly, quietly, strongly...
- **Prepositions** (preposiciones): of, for, at, on, in, under...
- **Conjunctions** (conjunciones): and, or, yet, but, what, if...
- **Verbs** (verbos): am, have, goes, worked, eaten...

Let's see one example in one sentence:

Wow! That gray dog that she bought in Germany runs fast!
INTERJ. DET. ADJ. NOUN CONJ PRON. VERB PREP. NOUN   VERB ADVERB

Each of these nine types identifies one function, but one same word can have different roles in different sentences. In the following example, the word "milk" has different uses (i.e. it functions as different types)

Noun:	**Milk** is the product from cows.
Adjective	**Milk** products sell well.
Verb:	The farmers **milk** the cows everyday.

Grammatical words are: determiners, pronouns, prepositions, conjunctions, a few adverbs, and the auxiliary verbs (to have, to be and to go). **Non-grammatical words** are: interjections, nouns, adjectives, most adverbs and verbs.

The following table displays the most important features of each type of words.

Type	Grammatical Words?	Masculine / femenine	Singular / plural	Person & tense
Interjections	no	no	no	no
Determiners	yes	yes	yes	no
Adjectives	no	yes	yes	no
Nouns	no	yes **	yes	no
Pronouns	yes	yes	yes	no
Adverbs	a few *	no	no	no
Prepositions	yes	no	no	no
Conjunctions	yes	no	no	no
Verbs	a few *	no	no	yes

(*) Because of their grammatical value we can consider grammatical words adverbs like "muy" (= very), "aquí" (= here), and the four auxiliary verbs: "ser," "estar" (both meaning "to be"), haber (= to have) and "ir" (= to go).

(**) Nouns have an intrinsic gender. They have a fixed gender: either masculine or feminine. Other types, for example determiners, have both.

As explained in the previous chapter, words can be classified into types (nouns, verbs, etc.) as per their function in the sentence. All types have their own rules.

The following are the definitions and elementary rules of the nine types of words.

Interjections

Interjections are those expressive words that constitute a sentence by themselves: Wow, Ah, Ouch, OK, Bye, etc. They are invariable.

Golden Rule

Interjections make up sentences by themselves, and they are invariable. They don't change regardless of occurring in the past, present or future, or for having one subject or another. As a consequence, each interjection is to be learned as is, with no further analysis.

For example, the English expression "Wow!" means "I am surprised by that," regardless of the context being in the present, past or future; regardless of who speaks (one or more people, masculine or feminine, etc.). Conversely, the equivalent sentence "I am surprised by that" is formed by pieces (each word) that are subject to grammar rules to be combined and have different meanings: "I was surprised by that," "He is surprised by that..."

Determiners

The determiners are those words that complement the noun, as: the, a, some, this, our... In Spanish, unlike the adjectives (which also qualify the noun), determiners go before the noun.

> [The] difficult lesson
> DET. ADJ.   NOUN

> [La] lección difícil
> DET. ADJ. NOUN

Golden Rule

> All determiners go before the noun, and they correspond to the noun in number (singular/plural) and in gender (masculine/ feminine).

For example, the translation of the English THE is the following:

> the boy/ the girl / the boys /the girls
> **el** niño /**la** niña/ **los** niños / **las** niñas

Adjectives

The adjectives are the words that inform us about qualities of the noun e.g. blue, large, expensive, happy, etc. Words like "tired" function as adjectives, although derived from verbs ("to tire").

Golden Rule

> Adjectives correspond with the noun in number (singular/plural) and in gender (masculine/feminine). They go after the noun, with some exceptions.

Unlike English, Spanish adjectives must correspond with their noun in number and gender. Example, "automático:"

>an automatic watch; some automatic watches
>un reloj automático, unos relojes automáticos

>an automatic machine; some automatic machines
>una máquina automática, unas máquinas automáticas

The exceptions are: "buen" (= good) "mal"(= bad), "primer" (= first), "tercer" (= third), and "gran" (=great).

Unlike English, Spanish can't create adjectives out of nouns. For example, "kidney" is a noun, but in the expression "kidney failure," it functions as a adjective.

Spanish can do something similar by using "de" (= of):

>**kidney** failure
>fallo del **riñón**

In addition, English and Spanish can also use the corrresponding adjective:

>renal failure
>fallo renal

Nouns

Nouns are all words that represent entities, such as persons, animals, plants, objects, places or ideas. For example: Jose, woman, zebra, pear, California, milk, love, velocity.

Golden Rule

All nouns in Spanish have an intrinsic gender regardless of whether or not they denote persons, animals or objects. (Words ending in "o" are more likely to be masculine; ending in "a", feminine). In addition, when we refer to more than one element, nouns add an "s" (or "es" if the word doesn't end in: a, e, i, o, u).

Examples:

José [masc.], mujer [fem.], cebra [fem.], pera [fem.], California [fem.], leche [fem.], amor [masc.], velocidad [fem.]

(= Jose, woman, zebra, pear, California, milk, love, velocity)

un carro, dos carros, un computador, dos computadores
one car, two cars, one computer, two computers

Pronouns

Pronouns are those words that substitute for a noun. Thanks to them, when the subject of the sentence is known, you avoid repeating the noun:

Instead of saying: **Mary** said **Mary** bought **the car**, now **the car** is **Mary's.**
We say: **She** said **she** bought **it**, now **it** is **hers.**

In English:

Personal pronouns	Possessive pronouns	Reflexive pronouns	Object pronouns
I	mine	myself	me
you	yours	yourself	you
he, she, it	his, hers, its	himself, herself, itself	him, her, it
we	ours	ourselves	us
you	yours	yourselves	you
they	theirs	themselves	them

In Spanish:

Personal Pronouns (*1)	Possessive pronouns (*2)	Reflexive Pronouns (*3)		Object Pronouns (*4)
yo	mío	a mí mismo/a ,	me	me, mí , conmigo
tú	tuyo	a ti mismo/a,	te	te, ti, contigo
él, ella	suyo/a	a él/ella mismo/a ,	se	lo, la, le, se , él, ella
nosotros/as	nuestro/a	a nosotros mismos/as,	nos	nos, nosotros
vosotros/as	vuestro/a	a nosotros mismos/as,	os	os, vosotros
ellos/as	suyo/a	a ellos/as mismos /as,	se	los, las, les, se, ellos/as

Notes:

(*¹) For clarity, the personal pronouns "usted" and "ustedes"are not in the
table. They mean you, singular and plural respectively; but they
follow the verb as if they were "él" and "ellos", respectively.

He is Perivian and **you are** Chilean.
Él es peruano y **usted es** chileno.

(*²) Don't confuse possessive pronouns (mine, yours, etc.) with
possessive determiners:

English	Spanish
my	mi
your	tu, su (= de usted)
his, her, its	su
our	nuestro
your	vuestro (Spain), su (de ustedes)
their	su

(*³) In Spanish reflexive pronouns can be simple (me, te, etc.) or
redundant (a mí mismo, a ti mismo, etc.). If you use the redundant
form, you have to use both.

Have you seen **yourself** in the mirror?
¿**Te** has visto en el espejo?   –simple–
¿**Te** has visto en el espejo **a ti mismo**?   –redundant–

(*⁴) For the third persons (so, él, she, it, they), Spanish distinguishes two
types of direct pronouns: direct and indirect. For now, use this rule:
Use only "lo/ la" or "los/ las," and if you encounter two lo, la, los,
las; change the first one for "se."

I have seen **her** in the cafeteria.
La he visto en la cafeteria.

I have written it **to them**.
Se lo he escrito. (instead of ~~Los lo~~ he escrito)

When the pronoun is preceded by a preposition different from "con"
(= with), the pronouns are: mí, ti, él, nosotros, vosotros ellos.

When the pronoun is preceded by the preposition "con" (=with), the
pronouns are: conmigo, contigo, (con) él/rlls, (con) nosotros, (con)
vosotro, (con) ellos.

Golden Rule

> **Personal pronouns** are normally omitted. **Possessive pronouns** are normally placed the same way as English. **Reflexive and Object pronouns** can normally go in the beginning of the sentence.

Examples:

> **I** am at home.
> (yo) Estoy en casa.
>
> This house is **mine.**
> Esta casa es **mía.**
>
> I am washing **myself.**
> (yo) **Me** estoy lavando.
>
> He is going to see **me** tomorrow.
> (Él) **me** va a ver mañana.
>
> This is for **me.**
> Esto es para **mí.**
>
> He is coming with **me.**
> (Él) está viniendo **conmigo.**

Adverbs

Adverbs answer the questions: how, where and when. Unlike adjectives, which give information about nouns, adverbs give information about verbs.

> They are reducing the cost of the product effective**ly.**
> Están reduciendo el coste del producto eficaz**mente.**

Golden Rule

> Adverbs function in a similar way as adjectives. The main difference is that adverbs are invariable: They don't change masculine/feminine or singular/plural.

Example:

> **Pedro** está trabajando **eficazmente. María** está trabajando **eficazmente.**
> **Pedro** is working **effectively. Maria** is working **effectively.**

Prepositions

Prepositions are grammatical words: they don't have a "tangible" meaning, only a structural value in the sentence they are in. They can be single-word prepositions: at, in, on, over, under, below, etc., or multiple-word expressions functioning as prepositions, as "on top of, " or "in the middle of."

Golden Rule

> Prepositions always link parts of the sentence, and they can never go at the end of the sentence. Unlike English, they are never a part of a verb.

For example:

> I am <u>calling **off**</u> the meeting for you.
> Estoy cancelando la cita para ti

> What are you <u>looking **for**</u>?
> ¿Qué estás <u>buscando</u>?

Conjunctions

Conjunctions are grammatical words that join two elemental clauses to create a compound sentence:

> <u>I studied enough.</u> |and| <u>I passed the test.</u>
> CLAUSE 1   CLAUSE 2

Golden Rule

> The translation English-Spanish is quite straightforward. For example, in every instance that you use "and," you can translate it by "y."

Verbs

Verbs are the nuclei of the sentence. A sentence can lack nearly anything but a verb. Verbs are all those words that describe what the subject (the person or thing) does. The simplest form of a verb is called "infinitive." The infinitive is also the representative form of the verb. In English it is preceded by the word "to;" in Spanish it always ends in –ar, -er, -ir.

> to repeat, to posses, to declare, to prefer, to toast
> repet**ir**, pose**er**,   declar**ar**, prefer**ir**, tost**ar**

Other that the infinitive (and two more), the tenses of the verbs change according to the subject: I, you, he, she, etc.

Golden Rule

The personal pronouns (yo, tú, él, etc.) are normally omitted because the verb contains that information in its ending. These endings are:

English	Spanish	Example
I	–VOWEL or –y	plane**o**, so**y** (= **I** plan, **I** am)
you (singular)	–s	invita**s** (= **you** invite)
he/she/it	–VOWEL	cuent**a** (= **he/she/it** counts)
we	–mos	convence**mos** (= **we** convince)
you guys (Spain)	–is	aparecé**is** (= **you guys** appear)
you guys / they	–n	estudia**n** (=**you/ they** study)

General Vocabulary

Possessive pronouns

English	Spanish
mine	mío/ a
yours (singular)	tuyo/ a
his, hers, its	suyo/ a
ours	nuestro/ a
yours (plural) theirs -Spain-	vuestro/ a
yours (plural) theirs	suyo/ a

Object pronouns

English	Spanish
to/ at me	me
to/ at you (singular)	te
to/ at him, her, it	lo, la, le, se
to/ at us	nos
to/ at you (plural) -Spain-	os
to/ at you (plural), them	los, las, les, se

Pronouns with the preposition "con" (= with)

English	Spanish
with me	conmigo
with you (singular)	contigo
with him, her, it	con él, con ella
with us	con nosotros
with you (plural) -Spain-	con vosotros
with you (plural), them	con ustedes, con ellos/ as

Pronouns with other prepositions, e.g. para (= for)

English	Spanish
for me	por mí
for you (singular)	para ti
for him, her, it	para él, para ella
for us	para nosotros
for you (plural) -Spain-	para vosotros
for you (plural), them	para ustedes, para ellos/ as

Technical Vocabulary

HVAC (Heating, Ventilation and Air Conditioning) and Safety

Quantities

English	Spanish
HVAC	(la) climatización
heating	(la) calefacción
ventilation	(la) ventilación
air conditioning	(el) aire acondicionado
quantity	(la) magnitud
cold	frío
density	(la) densidad
energy	energía
enthalpy	entalpía
entropy	entropía
flow	(el) caudal, flujo
heat	(el) calor
heat capacity	(la) capacidad calorífica
specific heat capacity	(el) calor específico
humidity	(la) humedad
relative humidity	(la) humedad relativa
internal energy	energía interna
mass	masa
power	potencia
preasure	(la) presión
temperature	temperatura
volume	(el) volumen
work	trabajo

Devices

English	Spanish
device	dispositivo
air diffuser	(el) difusor (de aire)
ventilation grate	rejilla
burner	(el) quemador
chimney	chimenea
fireplace	chimenea
compressor	(el) compresor
condenser	(el) condensador
cooling tower	(la) torre de refrigeración
duct	conducto
evaporator	(el) evaporador
extractor	(el) extractor
fan	(el) ventilador
fan-coil	(el) *fan-coil*
heater	(el) calentador
gas main	acometida de gas
water main	acometida de agua
gas meter	(el) contador de gas
water meter	contador de agua
pipe	tubería
pump	bomba
radiator	(el) radiador
drainage	(el) desagüe, sumidero
manhole	boca de alcantarilla
sewer	alcantarilla, conducto de a.residuales
sewerage	(las) aguas residuales
sewer system	(la) red de alcantarillas, alcantarillado
septic tank	fosa séptica
sink	pila
tank	(el) tanque, depósito
tap	grifo
thermostat	termostato
toilet	inodoro
turbine	turbina
valve	válvula

Concepts

English	Spanish
concept	**concepto**
air conditioning	(el) aire acondicionado
Avogadro number	número de Avogadro
Boltzmann constant	constante de *Boltzmann*
gas constant (R)	constante de los gases
bypass	(el) baipás
psychrometric chart	(el) diagrama psicrométrico
sanitary how water	(el) agua caliente sanitaria
thermic load	carga (térmica)
thermodinamics	termodinámica

Safety

English	Spanish
safety	(la) **seguridad**
alarm	alarma
boots	(las) botas
fire extinguisher	(el) extintor
hydrant	(el) hidrante
hose	manguera
fire	incendio
glasses	(las) gafas
gloves	(los) guantes
harness	(el) arnés
hardhat	(el) casco
lab gown	bata
overall	mono, (el) overol
panic bar, crash bar	barra antipánico
protection	(la) protección
pull station	alarma de incendio
sensor	(el) sensor
smoke	humo
smoke detector	(el) detector de humos
sprinkler	(el) *sprinkler*
welding helmet	careta

12. NEGATIONS AND QUESTIONS
NEGACIONES Y PREGUNTAS

Negative Sentences

To convert a sentence into negative you just need to add the word "no" before the verb.

> That acrobatics does <u>not appear</u> possible.
> Esa acrobacia <u>no parece</u> posible.
>
> Juan is <u>not going</u> to cancel an interview.
> Juan <u>no va</u> a cancelar una entrevista.

In Spanish, you have to use a double negative. The exception is when the negative words: "nunca," "nadie," or "ninguno" (= never, nobody, none) are placed before the verb.

> Juan has **never** cancelled an interview.
> Juan **no** ha cancelado una entrevista **nunca**.[double negation]
> Juan **nunca** ha cancelado una entrevista. [single negation]
> **Nunca** Juan ha cancelado una entrevista. [single negation]
>
> Nobody administers that office.
> No administra esa oficina **nadie**.[double negation]
> **Nadie** administra esa oficina. [single negation]

Ninguno has three forms "ninguno," "ninguna" and "ningún." Use the latter when you name the object.

No patient has cancelled the appointment.
Ningún paciente ha cancelado la cita.

None has cancelled the apponinment.
Ninguno ha cancelado la cita.

Notice that sentences using "nunca," "nadie" or "ninguno/a" (or ningún) are singular.

Nobody administers that office.
Nadie administra esa oficina.
Nadie administran esa oficina.

Interrogative Sentences

Unlike English, converting a sentence into interrogative requires only to put the right intonation.

If the question has a question word (what, where, when, which, etc), the **subject** normally goes after the verb.

At what time is **the director** leaving the hospital?
¿A qué hora está saliendo del hospital **el director**?

Otherwise (when there's no interrogative word), the location of the **subject** is optional

Is **Carlos** going to study at the library?
¿**Carlos** va a estudiar a la biblioteca?
¿Va **Carlos** a estudiar a la biblioteca?
¿Va a estudiar **Carlos** a la biblioteca?
¿Va a estudiar a la biblioteca **Carlos**?

Interrogative-Negative Sentences

When a sentence is both negative and interrogative, the rules of above overlap.

Has Juan never canceled an interview?
¿Juan **no** ha cancelado una entrevista **nunca**?
¿Juan **nunca** ha cancelado una entrevista?
¿**Nunca** Juan ha cancelado una entrevista?

General Vocabulary

Adverbs for negations and questions

English	Spanish
yes	sí
if	si
no, not	no
never	nunca
nobody	nadie
none, no...	ninguno/ a, ningún
What...?	¿Qué ...?
Which...?	¿Cuál/ Cuáles...?
Who...?	¿Quién/ Quiénes...?
Where...?	¿Dónde...?
When...?	¿Cuándo...?
How...?	¿Cómo ...?
How much...?	¿Cuánto/ a...?
How many...?	¿Cuántos/ as...?
(for) How long...?	¿(durante) Cuánto tiempo...?
How long ago...?	¿Cuánto tiempo hace que...?
How often...?	¿Con qué frecuencia...?
Since when...?	¿Desde cuándo...?

Technical Vocabulary

Mechanical tools and parts

Tools

English	Spanish
tool	heramienta
bar	barra
cable	(el) cable
chain	cadena
crane	grúa, pluma
drill	taladradora, taladro
drill bit	broca, barrena
file	lima
hammer	martillo
hook	gancho
jack	gato
ladder	escalera
link	(el) eslabón
machine tool	máquina herramienta
numerical control m.	máquina de control numérico
milling machine	fresadora
pickaxe	pico
pliers	(los) alicates
pulley	polea
rope	cuerda
screwdriver	(el) destornillador
flat-blade screwdriver	(el) destornillador plano
Phillip screwdriver	(el) destornillador de estrella
saw	sierra
circular saw	(la) radial
chain saw	motosierra
tape measure	cinta métrica
tongs	(las) tenazas
wedge	cuña
welder	(el) soldador
wheelbarrow	carretilla
wrench, spanner	(la) llave
Allen wrench	(la) llave *Allen*
adjustable wrench	(la) llave inglesa

Parts

English	Spanish
machinery	maquinaria
part	pieza
accelerator	(el) acelerador
axis	(el) eje
ball	bola
ball and socket joint	rótula
bearing	rodamiento
blade	(el) álabe, pala
brake	freno
cam	leva
chassis, frame	(el) chasis, (el) armazón, (el) bastidor
clutch	(el) embrague
combustion chamber	cámara de combustión
crank(shaft)	(el) cigüeñal
cylinder	cilindro
deposit	depósito
exhaust	tubo de escape
fastener	elemento de unión
screw	tornillo de punta
bolt	tornillo de tuerca
nut	tuerca
rivet	(el) remache
nail	clavo
washer	arandela
filter	filtro
gasket	junta
gear	(el) engranaje, marcha
hinge	bisagra
hopper	tolva
joint	(la) articulación
lever	palanca
motor	(el) motor
piston	(el) pistón
plug	bujía
propeller	(la) hélice
radiator	(el) radiador
spring	(el) muelle, (el) resorte
steering wheel	(el) volante

English	Spanish
tank	(el) tanque
tire	neumático
tooth	(el) diente
tread	rodamiento
valve	válvula
wheel, tire	rueda

SECTION IV

VERBS
VERBOS

So far you know three structures of verbs: I am singing, I have sung, and I am going to sing (Estoy cantando, He cantado, Voy a cantar). In this section we will add some verbs to shape some very useful structures (as those used to give instructions and recommendations).

You will learn that Spanish verbs can express: an action that falls on oneself (as in English in "I wash myself"), or an action without a subject (as in English in "Something appeals to me").

Later this section will introduce the present tense (I sing), and the past tense (I sang), and will give you some details on how to deal with the irregular verbs.

The last chapter, *Chapter 17 Next Steps in Spanish*, will provide you with a perspective on where you are in your learning: what you have learned, and what is ahead.

13. VERY IMPORTANT VERBS
VERBOS MUY IMPORTANTES

"Ser" and "Estar" (= to be)

Remember the conjugation of the verbs "ser" and "estar."

	ser	estar
(I)	soy	estoy
(you singular)	eres	estás
(he/she/it)	es	está
(we)	somos	estamos
(you guys)- Spain-	sois	estáis
(you guys/ they)	son	están

In *Chapter 9 One Future, Present, and Past*, you saw the forms of "estar" (estoy, estás, etc.) to build structures as: Estoy cantando (= I am singing); but this verb can also stand used alone, without another verb.

You will use "estar" as "to be" when the attribute is temporary, for example:

> **I am** content.
> **Estoy** contento.

But "to be" has another translation, "ser". The verb "ser" is used when the attribute is permanent.

> **I am** from Peru.
> **Soy** de Perú.

Warning

> Certain expressions that use "to be" in English, use another verb in Spanish: "tener."

For example:

> **I am** hungry/ thirsty/ hot/ cold/ sleepy/ twenty years old.
> **Tengo** hambre/ sed/ calor/ frío/ sueño/ veinte años.

Don't confuse the present tense you have studied (I am singing) with the "simple present" (I sing). The form "I am singing "combines the simple present of the verb "to be," with the gerund of the verb in question (here, to sing).

"Haber" and "Tener" (= to have)

Remember:

	haber	tener
(I)	he	tengo
(you singular)	has	tienes
(he/she/it)	ha	tiene
(we)	hemos	tenemos
(you guys) -Spain-	habéis	tenéis
(you guys/ they)	han	tienen

As explained *in Chapter 9 One Future, Present and Past*, the verb "haber" (he, has, ha, etc.) is an auxiliary verb, and it does not have a meaning. It is just used to build structures as: He cantado (= I have sung).

> **He** establecido un récord.
> **I have** established a record.

On the contrary, "tener," although it's equivalent "to have," has a concrete meaning, as "to have got."

> **Tengo** [tener] un problema
> **I have** a problem.

The expression "I have to" in Spanish uses the verb "tener," not "haber."

> I've got to cancel the tickets.
> Tengo que cancelar los tiquets.

"Ir" (= to go)

Remember:

	ir
(I)	voy
(you singular)	vas
(he/she/it)	va
(we)	vamos
(you guys)- Spain-	vais
(you guys/ they)	van

As *Chapter 9 One Future, Presen, and Past* explained, the form of "ir" (voy, vas, etc.), to build structures as: Voy a cantar (= I am going to sing). But this verb can also be used alone, as a simple verb, for example:

> Voy a la oficina en carro.
> I go to the office by car.

"Hay" and "Queda" (= *there is* and *there is left*)

To express "there is/ there are," Spanish uses "hay."

> **There is** water in my car.
> **Hay** agua en mi carro.

"Hay" is an impersonal form of the verb "haber." Impersonal means that there's no person doing the action. To use other tenses as "there was" or "there will be," you simply have to use the pattern of the verb "haber ."

> **There was** water in my car.
> **Había** agua en mi carro.

> **There were** two doctors available at that time.
> **Había** dos doctores disponibles en ese momento.

> **There will be** a solution.
> **Habrá** una solución.

Likewise it is "queda"

> **There is** water **left** in the bottle.
> **Queda** agua en la botella.

There are lemons **left** in the basket.
Quedan limones en la cesta.

"Poder" (= can, may) and "tener que" (= to have to)

The following is a table with all forms in the present tense for "poder."

	poder
(I)	puedo
(you singular)	puedes
(he/she/it)	puede
(we)	podemos
(you guys)- Spain-	podéis
(you guys/ they)	pueden

As *Chapter 9 One Future, Present and Past* explained, how to build sentences in those three tenses, but this is not enough to express **commands and recommendations.**

As in English, Spanish has a tense to express commands, as "Come this way." But the simplest way to convey a message that implies an order or a recommendation is to use the equivalent of "can" and "to have to."

Thus, for example, "Come this way" will become: "Can you come this way;" and "Take this pill" will become: "You have to take this pill."

Can you come this way.
Puedes venir por aquí.

You have to take one pill every six hours.
Tienes que tomar una píldora cada seis horas.

Notice that some forms of "poder" have **ue** despite the infinitive (poder) has an **o:** puedo, puedes, etc.

"Deber" (= to ought to) and "necesitar" (= to need)

The following is a table with all forms in the simple present for "deber" and
"necesitar."

	deber	necesitar
(I)	debo	necesito
(you singular)	debes	necesitas
(he/she/it)	debe	necesita
(we)	debemos	necesitamos
(you guys)- Spain-	debéis	necesitáis
(you guys/ they)	deben	necesitan

These two verbs help build sentences to express **commands and
recommendations.**

> **You need** one pill every six hours.
> **Necesitas** una píldora cada seis horas.

> **You need** to take one pill every six hours.
> **Necesitas** tomar una píldora cada seis horas.

> **You ought to take** one pill every six hours.
> **Debes** tomar una píldora cada seis horas.

These two verbs are **regular**. This means that they follow the table of
Spanishendings with no exceptions. The following is the table of endings for the
simple present, for verb in AR, ER, IR:

	AR	ER	IR
(I)	o	o	o
(you singular)	as	es	es
(he/she/it)	a	e	e
(we)	amos	emos	imos
(you guys)- Spain-	áis	éis	ís
(you guys/ they)	an	en	en

Irregular Verbs

A verb is **regular** when follows exactly all the endings that correspond to its conjugation. If a given verb has one single irregularity in just one tense, it is enough to call it **irregular**.
To illustrate what an irregular verb is, let's compare the regular verb "deber" with the irregular verbs "tener" and "ser."

The following table shows one column with the endings of the regular verbs in ER in the present tense, and the other columns with the forms of the verb "deber" (regular), and "tener" and "ser" (both irregular)

	Endings of ER verbs	deber	tener	ser
(I)	o	debo	ten g o	so y
(you singular)	es	debes	t ie nes	er es
(he/she/it)	e	debe	t ie ne	es
(we)	emos	debemos	tenemos	s o mos
(you guys)- Spain-	éis	debéis	tenéis	s o is
(you guys/ they)	en	deben	t ie nen	s o n

Note: The shading corresponds to those forms that are irregular. The frame indicates the irregularity.

Appendix C Present Tense shows a tense will all its irregularities and you can see many oif these transformations.

General Vocabulary

The verb "poder" (= can, may)

English	Spanish
can, may	poder
I can	puedo
you (singular) can	puedes
he/she/it can	puede
we can	podemos
you guys can -Spain-	podéis
you guys/ they can	pueden

The verb "deber" (= to ought to)

English	Spanish
to be	deber
I ought to	debo
You (singular) ought to	debes
He/ She/ It ought to	debe
We ought to	debemos
You guys ought to -Spain-	debéis
You guys/ They ought to e	deben

The verb "necesitar" (= to need)

English	Spanish
to have	necesitar
I need	necesito
you (singular) need	necesitas
he/she/it needs	necesita
we need	necesitamos
you guys need -Spain-	necesitáis
you guys/ they need	necesitan

The only grammatical words among the verbs are the auxiliary verbs: to have (haber), to be (ser and estar), and to go (ir). When they act as auxiliary verbs they are a structural part of a sentence.

Technical Vocabulary

Project Management

English	Spanish
project management	**dirección de proyectos**
application	(la) aplicación
breakdown	(el) desglose
campus	(el) campus
construction	(la) construcción
construction works	obra
construction site	obra
work of art	obra de arte
work, effort	trabajo
job	trabajo
cost	(el) coste
diagram	(el) diagrama
document	documento
blueprint, drawing	plano
contract	contrato
draft	(el) borrador
insurance	seguro
license	licencia
manual	(el) manual
map	(el) mapa
plan	(el) plan
warranty	garantía
law	(la) ley
regulation	(la) regulación
instructions	(las) instrucciones
norm	norma
rule	regla
rules	reglamento
emergency	emergencia
act of God	causa de fuerza mayor
contingency	contingencia
unforeseen	(el) imprevisto

English	Spanish
experiment	experimento
laboratory	laboratorio
management	(la) dirección, (la) gestión
planning	(la) planificación
coordination	(la) coordinación
inspection	(la) inspección
follow-up	seguimiento
design	diseño
maintenance	mantenimiento
message	(el) mensaje, (la) comunicación
call	llamada
conversation	(la) conversación
email message	(el) *email*
fax message	(el) fax
letter	carta
letter of intent	carta de intención
meeting	(la) reunión
video conference	videoconferencia
method	método
move	mudanza
operation	(la) operación
organization	(la) organización
phase	(la) fase
probe	sonda
procedure	procedimiento
process	proceso
product	producto
production	(la) producción
program	(el) programa
project	proyecto
quality	(la) calidad
relocation	(la) reubicación
revision	(la) revisión
sample	muestra
section	(la) sección
security	(la) seguridad
sequence	secuencia
set	conjunto
system	(el) sistema

English	Spanish
task	tarea
team	equipo
board	mesa directiva
committee	(el) comité
department	departamento
division	(la) división
human resources	(los) recursos humanos
term	plazo
test	(el) test
test tube	probeta
transport	(el) transporte

14. TRANSLATING "IT APPEALS TO ME"
TRADUCIENDO "ME GUSTA"

The verbs of the family of "gustar" (= to appeal, to like) are those that are conjugated the other way round, and the indirect object functions as the subject of the clause, and vice versa. There are verbs like those in both Spanish and English.

> That idea appeals to **me** (not: ~~I appeal that idea~~).
> Esa idea **me** gusta. (not: ~~Yo gusto esa idea~~).

For the purpose of making an analogy, we translated "gustar" as to appeal; although its meaning is closer to "to like:"

> I like that idea
> Esa idea **me** gusta.

Another example of verbs of this type is "doler" (= to hurt)

> This needle is going to hurt you. (not: ~~You are going to hurt it~~)
> Esta aguja va a dolerte. (not: ~~Tú vas a dolerte esta aguja~~).

In order to use these verbs, you need to know the pronouns that substitute the person in the sentence. These are:

English	Spanish	English	Spanish
me	me	It appeals to me.	Me gusta.
you (singular)	te	It appeals to you.	Te gusta.
him/ her	le	It appeals to him.	Le gusta.
us	nos	It appeals to us.	Nos gusta.
you guys	os (Spain)	It appeals to you.	Os gusta.
you guys, them	les	It appeals to them.	Les gusta.

Notes:
1. Notice that this list contains basically the same pronouns we saw in *Chapter11 Grammar Rules.*
2. Remember that, when using "usted" and "ustedes", you have to use the forms "le" and "les."
3. Remember that always the content in the fifth cell of our six-cell tables refers to the equivalent "you guys" which is used only in Spain.

Both English and Spanish have a few verbs with this peculiarity of being conjugated in the reverse. The problem is that they are not the same. For example, the verb "gustar" (= to like):

> You are going to like tennis.
> Te va a gustar el tenis.

The Optional Emphasis in the Person

In *Chapter 7 Conjugation*, we learned to put the personal pronoun (yo, tú, él…) in a sentence to emphasize who does the action.

> "I" am going to have that responsibility.
> "Yo" voy a tener esa responsabilidad.

With verbs of the family of "gustar" when you want to put emphasis on the person that makes the action, you cannot use the personal pronoun (since the subject of the sentence is not the person but the "thing"). So, instead, you will use the expressions below in addition of the pronouns: me, te, le, etc.

Spanish	English
a mí	me
a ti	you
a él, a ella	him, her
a nosotros/ as	us
a vosotros/ as (Spain)	you
a usted, a ellos/ as	them

Example:

> Recently soccer is fascinating 'you,' not 'me.'
> Recientemente, **a ti** te está fascinando el fútbol, no **a mí**.

The order of the sentence

You can alter the order of subject and object, as long as the verb follows
the conjugation of the actual object.

> Esa idea me está atrayendo. = Me está atrayendo esa idea.
> That idea is attracting me. = It's attracting me, that idea.

> Not "Esa idea e̶s̶t̶o̶y̶ atrayendo" or "E̶s̶t̶o̶y̶ atrayendo esa idea."

Tips

Exercise

> The majority of verbs of the family of "gustar" are regular. By
> using the endings of the simple present and the General
> Vocabulary of this chapter, translate the sentences below.

	AR	ER	IR
(I)	o	o	o
(you singular)	as	es	es
(he/she/it)	a	e	e
(we)	amos	emos	imos
(you guys)- Spain-	áis	éis	ís
(you guys/ they)	an	en	en

> I like driving.
> I don't care if you like it or not.
> We are interested in investing in the market of plastics.
> Does the nomination surprise you?
> They love soccer.

Answers

> Me gusta manejar.
> No me importa si te gusta o no.
> Estamos interesados en (= Nos interesa) invertir en el mercado
> de los plásticos.
> ¿Te sorprende el nombramiento?
> Les encanta el fútbol.

General Vocabulary

Useful verbs of the *gustar* family

English	Spanish
to appeal to	atra<u>e</u>r *
to be afraid of	dar mi<u>e</u>do *
to be left, as in "There's one pill left"	qued<u>a</u>r
to be sore, as in "My neck is sore"	dol<u>e</u>r *
to care, as in "I don't care"	import<u>a</u>r
to dislike, as in "I dislike that plan"	disgust<u>a</u>r
to feel like	apetec<u>e</u>r *
to feel shame	dar * vergü<u>e</u>nza, p<u>e</u>na
to feel sorry	dar p<u>e</u>na *
to find, as in "I find this cheap"	parec<u>e</u>r *
to get annoyed	enoj<u>a</u>r
to get astonished	asombr<u>a</u>r
to get bothered	molest<u>a</u>r
to get fascinated	fascin<u>a</u>r
to get indignant	indign<u>a</u>r
to get offended	ofend<u>e</u>r
to get surprised	sorprend<u>e</u>r
to give motivation	motiv<u>a</u>r
to have an opinion about something	result<u>a</u>r
to have fun	divert<u>i</u>r *
to like someone/ to dislike someone	ca<u>e</u>r * bien/ mal
to like, as in "I like playing guitar"	gust<u>a</u>r
to love, as in "I love playing guitar"	encant<u>a</u>r
to panic	dar pánico *
to revolt	dar <u>a</u>sco *, repugn<u>a</u>r

(*) irregular verb

Notice that the infinitive of all verbs in Spanish end in "ar," "er,"
"ir," and the stress is always in the last vowel.

Technical Vocabulary

Accounting and Procurement

English	Spanish
accounting	(la) contabilidad
procurement, Purchasing	(las) compras
agreement	acuerdo
asset	activo
liability	pasivo
advance	anticipo
amortization	(la) amortización
amount (price)	(el) importe, (la) cantidad
appraisal	(la) tasación
bank	banco
benefit	beneficio
bill	factura
bonus	bono
budget	presupuesto
business plan	(el) plan de negocio
capital	(el) capital
change order	(la) orden de cambio
collection	cobro
company	empresa
contest	concurso
cost	(el) coste
deal	trato
dealer, salesman, vendor	(el) comercial, (el) vendedor
debt	deuda
delivery term	plazo de entrega
discount	descuento
entry	partida
estimate	estimado
finance	(las) finanzas
first payment	entrada
investment	(la) inversión
lease	(el) *lease*
loan	préstamo
lost	pérdida
lump item	partida alzada
measurement	(la) medición

English	Spanish
method of payment	forma de pago
money	dinero
mortgage	hipoteca
negotiation	(la) negociación
offer	oferta
overhead	(los) gastos generales
pay off	finiquito
payment, installment	pago, letra
price	precio
profit	ganancia
purchase	compra
purchase order	(la) orden de compra
real estate	(los) inmuebles, (los) bienes raíces
receipt	recibo
rent	(el) alquiler
residual value	(el) valor residual
sale	venta
savings	ahorro
scope of services	(el) alcance de los servicios
security deposit	depósito de seguridad
seller	(el) vendedor
stock	(el) *stock* , (el) almacén
taxes	(los) impuestos
unit	(la) unidad
unit price	(el) precio unitario
value	(el) valor
VAT	IVA (Impuesto del Valor Añadido)

15. REFLEXIVITY AND PASSIVE VOICE
REFLEXIVIDAD Y VOZ PASIVA

In this chapter we will analyze other roles that the pronouns (me, you, him, etc.) can play with verbs. These cases are:

1) Reflexivity. When the action falls on the same subject that does the action.

> Little Pedro washes himself.
> Pedrito **se** lava.

2) Passive Voice. When the object over which the action falls becomes the subject. Unlike English, Spanish inserts a pronoun.

> The car is washed.
> El carro **se** lava.

For clarity –and for you to practice- the examples in this chapter use extensively the present tense"I sing" instead of "I am singing."

Remember the table of endings of the present tense:

	AR	ER	IR
(I)	o	o	o
(you singular)	as	es	es
(he/she/it)	a	e	e
(we)	amos	emos	imos
(you guys)- Spain-	áis	éis	ís
(you guys/ they)	an	en	en

Reflexivity

With many verbs, one can act on oneself (I wash myself). When a verb functions this way it is called reflexive. Notice that these verbs can act on something in the same way that they can act on themselves.

Let's take the verb to bathe (= bañar) as an example. A person can either act on something (the Direct Object) or on oneself.

> I bathe my 3-month old baby. / I bathe myself (I have a bath)
> (yo) Baño a mi bebé de 3 meses. / Me baño.

When a verb acts on itself, we say that the verb, in that use, is reflexive. In its reflexive form, the infinitive adds the particle **-se**, e.g. bañar**se** (= to bathe oneself, to have a bath).

> Having a bath is a pleasure.
> Bañarse es un placer.
>
> They have a bath in the river.
> (ellos) Se bañan en el río.
>
> They bathe each other in the river.
> (ellos) Se bañan en el río.

For clarity, we will call "reflexive" all verbs that follow the pattern shown above. Strictly speaking, some of them are called "pronominal verbs," as "arrepentirse" (= to repent).

Reflexive verbs can be classified into four types.

Type One. Verbs that function as either reflexive or not depending on the direct object being oneself or something else.
Note: In Spanish you can use the reflexive pronoun and the object in the same sentence: Me lavo el pelo (I wash "myself" my hair). e.g. lavar (= to wash).

> I wash my car in the garage.
> Lavo mi coche en el garaje.
>
> I wash myself with very warm water.
> Me lavo con agua muy caliente.

Most of the verbs of this category behave the same in Spanish and English

Type Two. Verbs that function as either reflexive or non-reflexive optionally, depending on the speaker's style. Reflexive style is more colloquial or implies more affection, e.g. comer (= to eat).

> I eat my lunch in half an hour.
> Como mi almuerzo en media hora.

> I eat my lunch in half an hour.
> Me como mi almuerzo en media hora.

Examples are: morir, olvidar, caer, escapar (= to die, to forget, to fall, to escape).

Type Three. Verbs that can function as either reflexive or not depending on the meaning, e.g. empeñar (= to insist/ to pawn).

> He insists in going.
> (Él) se empeña en ir.

> I have to pawn my jewels.
> Tengo que empeñar mis joyas.

Another example is: negar/ negarse (to deny/ to refuse).

Type Four. Verbs that can only function as reflexive, e.g. quejar (= to complain).

> This doesn't work: I am going to complain.
> Esto no funciona: me voy a quejar.

Examples are: arrepentirse, fugarse, atreverse, suicidarse (= to repent, to flee, to dare, to commit suicide).

The Passive Voice

A sentence is in passive voice when you have swapped the subject with the object, e.g.:

The nurse controls the machine at distance. (ACTIVE VOICE)
   SUBJECT   OBJECT

The machine is controlled by the nurse at distance. (PASSIVE V.)
SUBJECT   OBJECT

Spanish also has that structure:

La enfermera controla la máquina a distancia.

La máquina es controlada por la enfermera a distancia

But Spanish prefers to use the pronoun "**se**" for this structure, and to omit the real subject (nurse).

The machine is controlled at distance.
La máquina se controla a distancia.

Or: Se controla la máquina a distancia.

It's believed that that method works.
Se cree que ese método funciona.

Tips:

Use of: To get/ become + Adjective/ Past Participle

Sentences that express a transition as: I get sick, I get nervous (versus I'm sick, I'm nervous) are commonly translated in Spanish by the verb "ponerse" (literally: to put oneself).

(yo) pongo, (tú) pones, (él) pone, (nosotros) ponemos, (vosotros) ponéis, (ellos) ponen
I put, you put, s/he puts, we put, you guys, they put.

I become sick. I get nervous.
Me pongo enfermo. Me pongo nervioso.

General Vocabulary

Some verbs that can function as reflexive

English	Spanish
to bathe someone	bañar
to bathe oneself	bañarse
to bore someone	aburrir
to get bored	aburrirse
to comb someone	peinar
to comb oneself	peinarse
to dress someone	vestir *
to get dressed	vestirse *
to dry someone or sth.	secar
to get dried	secarse
to get up someone	levantar (a alguien)
to get up	levantarse
to meet with someone	quedar con (alguien)
to stay	quedarse
to put	poner *
to put on (clothes)	ponerse *
to take away	quitar
to take off (clothes)	quitarse
to shave someone	afeitar
to shave oneself	afeitarse
to tire someone	cansar
to get tired	cansarse
to try, to taste	probar *
to try clothes on	probarse *
to upset someone	enojar
to get upset	enojarse
to wake up someone	despertar * (a alguien)
to wake up oneself	despertarse *
to wash someone	lavar
to wash oneself	lavarse

(*) irregular verb

Technical Vocabulary

Mathematics

Graphs and forms

English	Spanish
graph	**gráfico**
form	**forma**
angle	ángulo
solid angle	ángulo sólido
point, dot	punto
inflection point	punto de inflexión
cutting point	punto de corte
focus	foco
center	centro
vertex	(el) vértice
pole	polo
line	línea
line	recta
axis	(el) eje
asistote	asístota
generatrix	(la) generatriz
segment	segmento
height	altura
side	lado
circumference	circunferencia
radius	radio
diameter	diametro
curve	curva
arc	arco
sinusoid	(el) senoide
area	(el) área
plane	plano
section	sección
face	cara
triangle	triángulo
square	cuadrado
rectangle	rectángulo
circle	círculo

English	Spanish
semicircle	semicírculo
circular sector	(el) sector circular
ellipse	(la) elipse
oval	óvalo
base	(la) base
quadrant	(el) cuadrante
volume	(el) volumen
cylinder	cilindro
cone	cono
prism	(el) prisma
cube	cubo
sphere	esfera

Concepts

English	Spanish
concept	**concepto**
approximation	(la) aproximación
calculation	cálculo
coefficient	(el) coeficiente
comma (1,000),	coma
point (period 2.3)	punto
constant	(la) constante
correlation	(la) correlación
cycle	ciclo
dimension	(la) dimensión
e, 2.81…	e
equation	(la) ecuación
differential equation	(la) ecuación diferencial
factor	(el) factor
formulae	fórmula
frequency	frecuencia
inequality	(la) inecuación
infinitesimal	infinitésimo
infinite	infinito
length	(la) longitud

English	Spanish
mathematics	(las) matemáticas
algebra	(el) álgebra
arithmetic	aritmética
calculus	cálculo
statistical	estadística
geometry	geometría
trigonometry	trigonometría
number	número
figure	cifra
natural number	número natural
integer number	número entero
negative number	número negativo
real number	número real
decimal	número decimal
fraction	(la) fracción
irrational number	número irracional
imaginary number	número imaginario
complex number	número complejo
scalar	(el) escalar
vector	(el) vector
matrix	(la) matriz
determinant	(el) determinante
order of magnitude	(la) orden de magnitud
parameter	parámetro
percentage	(el) porcentaje
period	periodo
pi, π	(el) pi
proportion	(la) proporción
ratio	ratio
symbol	símbolo
variable	(la) variable
unknown	incógnita

Functions and operations

English	Spanish
operation	(la) operación
function	(la) función
sum, summation, addition	suma
subtraction	resta
multiplication	producto
division	(la) división
power	potencia
power 2, square	cuadrado
power 3, cube	cubo
root	(la) raíz
square root	(la) raíz cuadrada
cube root	(la) raíz cúbica
exponential	(la) exponencial
logarithm	logaritmo
decimal logarithm	logaritmo decimal
natural logarithm (Naperian)	logaritmo neperiano
sine	seno
cosine	coseno
tangent	(la) tangente
cotangent	cotangente
secant	(la) secante
cosecant	(la) cosecante
arcsine	arcoseno
arccosine	arcocoseno
arctangent	(la) arcotangente
arccotangent	(la) arcocotangente
arcsecant	(la) arcosecante
arccosecant	(la) arcocosecante
hyperbolic sine	seno hiperbólico
hyperbolic cosine	coseno hiperbólico
hyperbolic tangent	(la) tangente hiperbólica
hyperbolic cotangent	(la) cotangente hiperbólica
hyperbolic secant	(la) secante hiperbólica
hyperbolic cosecant	(la) cosecante hiperbólica
maximum	máximo
minimum	mínimo
average	media
variance	varianza

English	Spanish
normal distribution	(la) distribución normal
covariance	(la) covarianza
limit	(el) límite
derivative	derivada
second derivative	segunda derivada
integral	(la) integral
double integral	(la) integral doble
triple integral	(la) integral triple
Taylor series	(la) serie de *Taylor*
transform	transformada

16. THE PRESENT AND PAST TENSES
LOS TIEMPOS PRESENTE Y PASADO

So far you have learned three tenses. Let's review this with the verb "to sing." We have one present (I am singing), one past (I have sung), and one future (I am going to sing).

These three tenses are compounded and are formed with more than one verb.

I am singing	(to be + to sing)
I have sung	(to have + to sing)
I am going to sing	(to be + to go + to sing)

These tenses are the simplest. Once you know the auxiliary verbs involved (the equivalents in Spanish to "to be," "to have," and "to go"), you don't need much more.

Paradoxically, the simple tenses (those that involve only one verb) are more difficult, because you have to deal with the irregularities of the verb that you are using (and there are many verbs).

In this chapter we will see:

- the **regular** verbs in the **present tense** (I sing)
- the **regular** verbs in the **past tense** (I sang)
- the **false-irregular** or spelling-changing verbs
- the **irregular** verbs

Regular Verbs in the Present Tense

The following is the table of endings of the present tense of the regular verbs.

	AR Verbs	ER Verbs	IR Verbs
(I)	-o	-o	-o
(you singular)	-as	-es	-es
(he/she/it)	-a	-e	-e
(we)	-amos	-emos	-imos
(you guys)- Spain-	-ais	-eis	-ís
(you guys/ they)	-an	-en	-en

When you apply those endings to the three model verbs, the result is:

	cantar	beber	partir
(I)	canto	bebo	parto
(you singular)	cantas	bebes	partes
(he/she/it)	canta	bebe	parte
(we)	cantamos	bebemos	partimos
(you guys)- Spain-	cantáis	bebéis	partís
(you guys/ they)	cantan	beben	parten

We marked the person in parentheses to indicate that, in Spanish, it is redundant. You don't need to say: "Yo canto" (= I sing), just "Canto."

Examples of use of the present tense:

> I sing, you sing, he sings, we sing, you guys sing, you/ they sing
> canto, cantas, canta, cantamos, cantáis (Spain), cantan
>
> I drink, you drink, he drinks, we drink, you drink, you/they drink
> bebo, bebes, bebe, bebemos, bebéis (Spain), beben
>
> I live, you live, he lives, we live, you guys live, you/they live
> vivo, vives, vive, vivimos, vivís (Spain), viven

Unlike English, Spanish can use the present tense to describe historical facts.

> Columbus discovered America in 1492.
> Colón descubre America en 1492.

Regular Verbs in the Past Tense

The following is the table of endings of the present tense of the regular verbs.

	AR Verbs	ER Verbs	IR Verbs
(I)	-é	-í	-í
(you singular)	-aste	-iste	-iste
(he/she/it)	-ó	-ió	-ió
(we)	-amos	-imos	-imos
(you guys) - Spain-	-asteis	-isteis	-isteis
(you guys/ they)	-aron	-ieron	-ieron

When you apply those endings to the three model verbs, the result is:

	cantar	beber	partir
(I)	canté	bebí	partí
(you singular)	cantaste	bebiste	partiste
(he/she/it)	cantó	bebió	partió
(we)	cantamos	bebimos	partimos
(you guys) - Spain-	cantasteis	bebisteis	partisteis
(you guys/ they)	cantaron	bebieron	partieron

False-irregular or Spelling-changing Verbs

It may happen that the verb needs to alter its spelling to accommodate the right pronunciation. An example is **vencer** (= to defeat). If we add the endings to form the present tense, we obtain a wrong pronunciation of its forms. Venc-er /benthér/ → it should sound /benth-o/, but ~~venco~~ gives /benko/ instead.

	vencer
(I)	venzo
(you singular)	vences
(he/she/it)	vence
(we)	vencemos
(you guys)-Spain-	vencéis
(you guys/ they)	vencen

If you take the stem venc- and then add the suffix -o, the result is venco, but the "c" with "o" doesn't sound as "s" of vencer. That's why the spelling needs to change.

This happens with the verbs ending in:

                -cer → -zo
                -cir → -zo
                -ger → -jo
                -gir   → -jo
                -guir → -go
                -quir → -co

Warning

> You don't have to memorize these endings. As you learn the rules of spelling of this book, you will notice when you write them (remember: pronunciation wise, they are regular). Notice that it is the same tranformation of:
> poco (= little of) + ito → poquito (= little bit of), not ~~pocito~~

Examples:

	-cer → -zo	**-cir → -zo**	**-ger → -jo**
	vencer	esparcir	proteger
	= to defeat	= to spread	= to protect
(I)	venzo	esparzo	protejo
(you singular)	vences	esparces	proteges
(he/she/it)	vence	esparce	protege
(we)	vencemos	esparcimos	protegemos
(you guys)-Sp.	vencéis	esparcís	protegéis
(you guys/ they)	vencen	esparcen	protegen

	-gir → jo	**-guir → -go**	**quie → -co**
	exigir	distinguir	delinquir
	= to demand	= to distinguish	= to commit a crime
(I)	exijo	distingo	delinco
(you singular)	exiges	distingues	delinques
(he/she/it)	exige	distingue	delinque
(we)	exigimos	distinguimos	delinquimos
(you guys)-Sp.	exigís	distinguís	delinquís
(you guys/ they)	exigent	distinguen	delinquen

Also notice that these alterations can also happen when the verb is irregular for other reasons. For example "seguir" (= to follow) is irregular (not what we called "false irregular"). The present tense "sigo" (I follow) changes its stem; and in addition, it needs to alter its "u" to accommodate to the right pronunciation, according to the above rules ("sigo," not ~~siguo~~).

These alterations only take place with the Present tense and Present Subjunctive (Present Subjunctive is not covered in this book).

The Irregular Verbs

Remember what we saw in *Chapter 7 Conjugation,* the infinitive (as "to sing") is the prime form of the verb and also its representative.

Every variation of a verb is called "the form" of the verb. Thus, for example, the infinitive "to sing" has several forms: sing, sang, sung. In Spanish, verbs have many forms.

Remember that all Spanish infinitives end in AR, ER, IR, with no exception. What is left in the verb when you remove AR, ER, IR is called the stem. Thus, **the stems** of the verbs: cant**ar**, beb**er**, and viv**ir** (to sing, to drink, to live) are: cant, beb, viv.

Each form of a verb can be broken down into two parts: the stem and the ending.

> canto = cant + o   (I sing)
> cantamos = cant + aremos (We sing)

A form can be irregular for three different reasons: 1) because the stem changes, 2) because the ending changes, or 3) because both change.

In the intermediate course *Spanish for Californians: Using English to Learn Spanish* you will learn about irregular verbs in detail. For now, **what is important is that you learn how to recognize the infinitive** out of any form you hear (in order to identify its meaning or to be able to find its meaning in the dictionary). For example, imagine you know the word "pintar" (= to paint), and your patient says: "Pintamos casas" (= We paint houses), you should recognize, a least, the infinitive "pintar."

For this purpose, the following classification of irregular forms will be
helpful:

- **Irregular form because of changes in its ending**

  A form can be irregular due to a transformation of its ending.
  For example the present tense of "distribuir" is "distribuyo," not
  ~~distribuo~~." The stem "distribu" hasn't changed.

  Since here the stem doesn't change, you should have no
  problem to recognize its infinitive ("distribuir").

- **Irregular form because of changes in its stem**

  A form can be irregular due to a transformation of its stem.
  There are two very common transformations (from what it
  should be if regular to what really is) **o → ue** and **e → ie**. For
  example the present tense of contar (= to count) is "c**ue**nto" (I
  count) , not "~~conto~~." Another example: the present tense of the
  verb preferir (= to prefer) is "pref**ie**ro (= I prefer), not "~~prefero~~."

  Knowing this should help you **recognize the infinitive** of the
  form. Now, if you hear forms as "cuento" or "prefiero," you can
  expect than the infinitives will be "contar," and "preferir." And
  remember: the form that you will find in the dictionary is the
  infinitive (contar = to count; preferir = to prefer).

- **Irregular form because of changes in both, ending and stem**

  A form can be irregular due to a transformation of both ending
  and stem. There are only three verbs with forms having an
  unrecognizable infinitive: haber, ser, and ir. Thus, for example,
  from the forms "he" (= I have just…), eres (= you are), or voy
  (= I go), you cannot deduce that their infinitives are: "haber,"
  "ser," or "ir," respectively. This is why you should get very
  familiar with these verbs .

	haber	ser	ir
(I)	he	soy	voy
(you singular)	has	eres	vas
(he/she/it)	ha	es	va
(we)	hemos	somos	vamos
(you guys)- Spain-	habéis	sois	vais
(you guys/ they)	han	son	van

General Vocabulary

General Questions

We recommend that you learn some useful sentences that can't be
translated literally. Learn each structure as is.

What's your name? My name is Antonio Smith.
¿Cómo te llamas? Me llamo Antonio Smith.

How old are you? I'm 40 years old.
¿Cuántos años tienes? Tengo 40 (cuarenta) años.

Where are you from? I'm from San Jose, California.
¿De dónde eres? Soy de San José, California.

How long have you been here? I've been here for 3 years / I've
been here since 2009.
¿Cuánto tiempo llevas aquí? Llevo aquí tres años. / Llevo aquí
desde el 2009.

How long ago did you work there?
¿Cuánto hace que trabajaste allí?

How often do you take your medicine?
¿Con qué frecuencia tomas tu medicina?

What's the time?
¿Qué hora es?

What's your date of birth?
¿Cuál es tu fecha de nacimiento?

What's your telephone?
¿Cuál es tu teléfono?

Notice that all these sentences above use the conjugation of "tú" (you-
informal) as in "¿Cómo te llamas?", instead of "usted", as in "¿Cómo se
llama?" . The phasebook at the end of this volume, uses "usted" (you-
formal), to expose you to that form.

Technical Vocabulary

The Office and the Travels

The office

English	Spanish
office	oficina
address	(la) dirección
binder	carpeta
blog	(el) blog
branch	sucursal
building	edificio
business card	tarjeta
cabinet	armario
calendar	calendario
camera	cámara
cellular	(el) celular, (el) móvil
chair	silla
chief	(el/la) jefe
computer	(el) ordenador, (el/la) computador/a
coverage	cobertura
coworker	(el/la) compañero/a
customer	(el) cliente
desk	escritorio, mesa
document	documento
door	puerta
email	(el) email
employee	empleado
file	archivo
folder	carpeta
headquarters	(la) sede, (la) central, (las) oficinas centrales
internet conection	(la) conexión de internet
meeting room	sala de reunión
paper	(el) papel
pass	(el) pase, (la) autorización
pen	bolígrafo
photo	(la) foto
radio	(el) radio, (la) radio
recepcionist	(el/la) recepcionista
schedule	agenda, (el) programa

English	Spanish
secretary	(el/la) secretario/a
town hall	ayuntamiento
television	(la) televisión
timetable	calendario, horario
video	vídeo, video
website	sitio web
work	trabajo
work phone	teléfono en el trabajo
ZIP	código postal

Travels

English	Spanish
travel	(el) **viaje**
airport	aeropuerto
ambulance	(el) ambulancia
bag	bolso
bar	(el) bar
bed	cama
book	libro
box office	ventanilla, taquilla
breakfast	desayuno
bus	(el) autobús
cafeteria	cafetería
car	carro, (el) coche
cash	efectivo
cinema	(el) cine
clock	(el) reloj
coat	abrigo
credit card	tarjeta de crédito
currency	moneda
customs	aduana
dinner	cena
doctor	médico
drink	bebida
driving carner	(el) carnet de conducir

English	Spanish
fire fighters	bomberos
freeway, highway	autopista
flight	vuelo
food	comida
glasses, spectacles	(las) gafas, (los) lentes
hospital	(el) hospital
hotel	(el) hotel
insurance	seguro, seguranza
key	(la) llave
luggage	(el) equipaje
medicine	medicina
menu	(el) menú
news	(las) noticias
newspaper	periódico
passport	(el) pasaporte
plane	(el) avión
police	policia
briefcase	(el) maletín
restaurant	(el) restaurante
room	(la) habitación
shop	tienda
station (bus, train)	(la) estación
street	(la) calle
street map	plano
suit	(el) traje
taxi	(el) taxi
ticket	(el) billete, (el) tiquet
train	(el) tren
transportation	(el) transporte
watch	(el) reloj
waiter	camarero
wallet	cartera
underground, subway	metro

17. NEXT STEPS IN SPANISH
PASOS SIGUIENTES EN EL ESPAÑOL

What have you learned

These are the skills you have:

- **You can read**. You may not understand everything you read, but you can read every quick note in Spanish. On the spot, when talking with someone, you can communicate a certain word you don't know by using your pocket dictionary and be able to read it properly.

- **You can write**. You may misspell words (~~pasiente~~ instead of paciente; or ~~ora~~ instead of hora), but everything you write will be understandable. On the spot, you can memorialize data (directions, a prescription, etc.).

- **You can use the dictionary efficiently**. You can find words quickly in your future learning. You can also convert texts or quick notes no matter which changes are in the words, no matter the word being feminine (e.g. amarilla instead of amarillo -yellow) , plural (e.g. carros instead of carro –cars vs. car) or a conjugated form (e.g. "canto" instead of "cantar" – I sing vs. to sing).

- **You can greet and express immediate messages**. You know many stand alone sentences as: hola, adiós, uno, sí, cuidado, or okey (= hello, goodbye, one, yes, watch out, OK)

- **You can make statements and questions about the past, present, and future**. You may not understand the tense of your speaker yet, but you can convey any message and "conjugate" in a past, present, or future tense.

- **You can give instructions and recommendations.** You can use the equivalents of "to need," "to have to" and "can."

This gives you enough tools to start communicate in the context of a health care provider that addresses a patient, but most importantly, this knowledge is the foundation of Spanish.

What to remember

The Spanish in this book is not all of it. It is limited to the technical setting. It is good that you know your strengths:

- **You control the conversation**. You are the one that asks the questions, so you can set the language level of the conversation. For instance, if you use the tense "Have you done…?" the speaker will tend to answer the same way ("Yes, I have done…or I haven't done…" (instead of "I did").

  This is why this book focuses on those tenses that are the simplest to learn and use.

- **You know the context.** You know the protocol of a technical visit, from the greeting to the departure.

  This is why this volume includes a phrasebook sorted by the settings: 1) getting the patient's history, 2) examining and diagnosing, 3) procedures and treatments, and 4) teaching and follow up.

- **You are a health care professional already.** You are the one that knows the message that needs to be conveyed to the patient.

  For this reason the method of this book doesn't impose the words you are going to learn. You are the one that knows what needs to be asked and said to the patient.

- **You can speak English already**. English has many commonalities with Spanish. Many Spanish words (technical and non technical) are similar to their English counterpart. In addition, the patient may know some English; so, with caution, words in English can be used as a last resource.

  This is why this book: is in English, uses similar words in English in its examples, and has lists of words in alphabetical order in English.

- **You can always ask the patient.** You can ask the patient to repeat or to put in writing the words you didn't catch.

  This is one of the reasons why the first chapters of this book teach you how to read and write first.

- **You know the basic Spanish you need.** You don't need to know words of slang or any deviation of the language. If the patient doesn't speak a standard Spanish, you must request a professional interpreter (who may also struggle).

  This is why this book only uses normative Spanish: the standard used in all Spanish-speaking countries.

- **You know the basic technical Spanish you need.** You don't need a very technical vocabulary. The patients don't know technical terms. The words you need to acquire are just those that you expect to use and hear with your patients.

  This is why this book focus just in that Spanish heard in technical settings; and it provides just the vocabulary in the health field that a patient commonly knows and understand.

What is out there

We have identified **six elements that** can be obstacles in learning for the English-speaker.

1. Objects have gender (*Chapter 6 Masculine/ Feminine*).
2. There are two verbs for "to be;" "ser" and "estar" (*Chapter7 Conjugation*).
3. Verbs are conjugated; and some verbs are irregular (*Chapter7 Conjugation*).
4. Pronouns can appear in pairs - I will tell <u>that</u> to <u>him</u> (*Chapter 11 Grammar Rules*).
5. There are two types of past tense: the preterite and the imperfect past. E.g. "I **sang** yesterday" vs. "I **used to sing**").
6. There are two extra tenses; they are called the present subjunctive and the past subjunctive. E.g. "It is important that you **are** here tomorrow" vs. "It is important that you **be** here tomorrow").

After completion of this book, the natural next step would be a grammar course at the intermediate level. We recommend the book *Spanish for Californians*, where you will learn:

- **More Grammar Structures.**

   What this book calls "rules of thumb" have exceptions. For example the rule of thumb that the pronouns can be placed in front of the verb is true, but in some cases, they can be placed after the verb.

   I am going to need **him** tomorrow.
   Lo voy a necesitar mañana [option 1].
   Voy a necesitar**lo** mañana   [option 2].

   In this regard, the book *Spanish for Californias: Using English to Learn Spanish* devotes one chapter for each part of the speech (nouns, adjectives, verbs, etc.).

- **More Verbal Tenses**

You will learn different ways to communicate ideas in the present, past or future. This book limits itself to one form for each tense (The equivalents of: "I am doing." "I have done," "I am going to do"). These are the simplest in Spanish; there are others. For example

> I **am going to** need him tomorrow.
> Lo voy a necesitar mañana.
>
> I **will** need him tomorrow.
> Lo necesitaré manana.

This includes the tenses that become more problematic in Spanish: **the subjuctive tenses.**

> I am going to suggest that he **use** it. (vs. "uses")
> Voy a sugerir que lo **use** (vs. "usa")

The book *Spanish for Californians* analyzes the use of each verb tense, classifies its irregularities, as well as it provides a table with the irregular verbs and its types of irregularities.

Tips

Frequently Asked Questions

FAQ 1: Where can I find sentences to practice?

> Nowadays, there are many free resources available online; but the simplest is the Phrasebook in this book. These phrases are consistent with what you have learned in this book.

FAQ 2: Where can I learn about dialects and cultural differences?

> There are two appendices at the end of this book focusing on the three major dialectal variations within Spanish language (Spain, Latin America, and Argentina), and some cultural features that Spanish-speaking countries have in common.

General Vocabulary

Verbs

Since verbs are not grammatical words (with the exception of the auxiliary verbs as: ser, estar or haber), they are not part of the General Vocabulary of this book. However, there is a group of irregular verbs that are paradigms in the conjugations of Spanish verbs, and consequently, you will need to learn them as part of the conjugation (this is, part of the grammar).

Another reason to learn these verbs is also practical. Most of them are very used and useful.

Notice that the verbs mentioned in *Chapter 10 Irregularities in the Future, Present and Past*, are included in the list below.

English	Spanish
to ask for	pedir (*[1])
to be (temporal)	estar
to be (permanent)	ser
to be worth	valer
to break	romper
to bring	traer
to build	construir (*[2])
to come	venir
to come cack	volver
to cover	cubrir
to die	morir
to do	hacer
to fall	caer
to fit	caber
to give	dar
to go	ir
to grow	crecer
to have	tener
to have (auxiliary)	haber
to hear	oír
to know	saber
to leave	salir
to let go	soltar
to meet (a norm)	satisfacer

English	Spanish
to open	abrir
to play	jugar
to power	poder
to produce	producir (*[3])
to put	poner
to resolve	resolver
to say	decir
to see	ver
to sleep	dormir (*[4])
to start	comenzar (*[5])
to walk	andar
to want	querer
to write	escribir

Notes

(*[1]) "Pedir" is the paradigm of the irregular verbs with an "e" in the second to last syllable transforming "e" into "i." This is explained in *Chapter 10 Irregularities in the Future, Present and Past* (Irregularities in the Gerund, Type 3).

(*[2])"Construir" is the paradigm of the irregular verbs ending in -aer, -eer, -oer, -oír, -uir. This is explained in *Chapter 10 Irregularities in the Future, Present and Past* (Irregularities in the Gerund, Type 1).

(*[3]) "Producir" is the paradigm of the irregular verbs ending in -cer, -cir.

(*[4]) "Dormir" is the paradigm of the irregular verbs with an "o" in the second to last syllable transforming "o" into "u." This is explained in *Chapter 10 Irregularities in the Future, Present and Past* (Irregularities in the Gerund, Type 2).

(*[5])"Comenzar" is the paradigm of the irregular verbs with an "e" in the second to last syllable transforming "e" into "ie."

Technical Vocabulary

Adjectives

Adjectives commonly used with "ser:" (permanent attributes)

English	Spanish
automatic	automático (e.g. El coche **es** automático.)
manual	manual
constructive	constructivo
cheap, unexpensive	barato
expensive	caro
colorful	de colores
white	blanco
gray	gris
black	negro
yellow	amarillo
red	rojo
dark red	rojo oscuro
light red	rojo claro
blue	azul
green	verde
orange	naranja
violet	violeta
brown	marrón
transparent	transparente
electrical, electric	eléctrico
electronic	electrónico
environmental	medioambiental
final	final
temporary	temporal
provisional	provisional
draft	borrador
financial	financiero
fiscal	fiscal
hydraulic	hidráulico
individual	individual
software	informatico, de *software*
legal	legal
regulatory	reglamentario
contractual	contractual

English	Spanish
linear, first-degree	lineal, de primer grado
quadratic, second-degree	cuadrático, de segundo grado
local	local
domestic	nacional
international	internacional
mechanical	mecánico
natural	natural
artificial	artificial
nuclear	nuclear
piecework	a destajo
pneumatic	pneumático
professional	profesional
personal	personal
quality	de calidad
ring-shaped	con forma de anillo
straight	recto
curved	curvo
triangular	triangular
squared	cuadrado
rectangular	rectangular
circular	circular
prismatic	primático
spherical	esférico
cilindrical	cilíndrico
conical	cónico
rental	en alquiler, de alquiler
owned	en propiedad
secondhand	de segunda mano
new, brand new	nuevo
short-term	a corto plazo
long-term	a largo plazo
standard	estándar
simple	simple
double	doble
multiple	múltiple
solar	solar
technical	técnico
thermal	térmico
turn-key	llave en mano

Note: As explained in *Chapter 11 Grammar Rules*, unlike
English, the Spanish adjectives are placed after the noun:

problema medioambiental
environmental problem

In addition to this, in most cases, you have the option to
mean the same using "de" (= of) and the corresponding
noun (In English the corresponding noun of "arterial" is
"artery"):

problema de medio ambiente
problem of environment

Adjectives commonly used with "estar:" (states)

English	Spanish
in trial	en pru<u>e</u>bas (e.g. La máquina **está** en pruebas)
in warranty	en garantía
parallel	en paral<u>e</u>lo
series	en s<u>e</u>rie
wireless	sin h<u>i</u>los, *wireless*

Note: All past participles (These are words as "broken," or
"fixed") can function as djectives if accompaning a noun.
For example, in "a broken car," broken accompanies the
noun "car." These adjectives are commonly used with the
verb "estar," since they typically define a "state."

El carro está roto. El carro está reparado.
The car is broken. The car is fixed.

You can check this rule in *Chapter 10 Irregularities in
Future, Present, and Past*, with the past participles shown
in the section Irregular Verbs in the Past Participle, as:
abierto (open), cubierto (covered), escrito (written), etc.

La puerta está abierta.
The door is open..

PHRASEBOOK

PHRASEBOOK

A phrasebook contains useful expressions and their translations. Some phrase include comments on the grammar, and they are an excellent form to test yourself.

The translations are not literal. The Spanish phrases resort to what you have learned in this book. Thus, for example #56 "Send it by email" is translated as ¿Puedes enviarlo por email? since the imperative tense (the commands) are not covered in this book. Likewise, the book sticks to the tenses "Voy a cantar" (I am going to sing), "He cantado" (I have sung), "Estoy cantando" (I am singing), and ocassionaly "Canto" (I sing).

1. **Hello, my name is Ana Alonso, with Intel. I am going to be working with you in this project.**
   Hola, me llamo Ana, de Intel. Voy a estar trabajando contigo en este proyecto.

   Note: "Me llamo" is literally "I call myself."

2. **My name is Antonia Agüero Vargas.**
   Me llamo Antonia Agüero Vargas.

   Notes: 1. In many Spanish-speaking countris it is costumary to use the two last names. 2. They may use the formal "usted" istead of "tú" (¿Como te llamas?). –See *Appendix B Notes About Culture.*

3. **What's your name?**
   ¿Cómo se llama (usted)?

   > Notes: 1. They may use the formal "usted" instead of "tú"
   > (¿Como te llamas?). –See *Appendix B Notes About Culture*.

4. **This is Pedro Alonso, with the City Hall.** -When introducing
   someone-
   Él es Pedro Alonso, del Ayuntamiento.

   > Note: You maynot translate "this" as "Éste," but ""el".

5. **This is Ana Pérez.** -When identifying oneself over the phone-
   Soy Pedro Alonso, del Ayuntamiento.

   > Note: You maynot translate "this" as "Éste," but "soy."

6. **I need to ask you some questions to write my follow-up report.**
   Necesito hacerte unas preguntas para escribir mi informe de
   seguimiento.

7. **Who is the consultant for the HVAC?**
   ¿Quién es el consultor de climatización?

8. **You will need a pass to enter the site.**
   Vas a necesitar un pase para entrar en la obra

   > Notes: 1. "Obra" has several translations. Other are the
   > "execution of a project," Va a ser una obra de dos años (It's
   > going to be a 2-year execution project).

9. **What is the address of the project site?**
   ¿Cuál es la dirección de la obra?

10. **24, 10th St., San Rafael, California.**
    Calle diez, número veinticuatro, San Rafael, California.

    > Notes: 1. You can expect that people will say first the street
    > number. 2.Rafael would be: /rah-fah-ehl/.

11. **How do you spell that?**
    ¿Cómo se deletrea?

     Note: Literally "How is it spelled?"

12. **Ana Hernández, as it sounds. With "z" and "h"**
    Ana Hernández, como suena. Con zeta y hache.

     Note: "s" sound can be spelt with "s," "z" or "c."

13. **Can you write that down?**
    ¿Lo puedes escribir?

14. **I don't know how to spell it in Spanish.**
    No sé cómo se deletrea en español.

     Notes: 1. Sé (with accent mark) is the present tense of "saber,"
     irregular. 2. "Se deletrea" means is "it is spelt" (see *Chapter 15
     Reflexivity and Passive Voice*).

15. **What is your phone number?**
    ¿Cuál es tu teléfono?

     Note: Literally "Which is your phone number?"

16. **My cell is, area code 510 676-1101.**
    Mi celular es código de área quinientos diez, seis siete seis, once
    cero uno.

     Note: You can expect different groupings of figures, as: cinco,
     uno, cero...

17. **Can you say one number at a time?**
    ¿Puede decir los números uno a uno?

18. **What is the date of the meeting?**
    ¿Cuál es la fecha de la reunión?

     Note: Literally "Which is your phone number?"

19. **March 2**
    "2/3" El dos de marzo.

    Note: 1. Literally "The two of march". 2. Make sure it is left clear
    what figure represents day and month –See *Appendix B Notes
    About Culture.*

20. **Which day is March 2?**
    ¿Qué día de la semana es el dos de marzo?

    Note: 1. Al alternative "¿Qué día cae el dos de marzo?, literally
    "Which day does it fall March 2?"

21. **Have you even been at the headquarters? No, I haven't**
    ¿Has estado en la central alguna vez? No.

    Note: The common response is "Sí" or "No." It's very uncommon
    to use tags as "No lo he estado" (No, I haven't), unless you want
    to enphasize the answers.

22. **I have never been there.**
    No he estado allí nunca.

    Note: Double Negative (see *Chapter 12 Negations and
    Questions*).

23. **I need your signature / initials.**
    Necesito su firma/ sus iniciales.

24. **This is information about your privacy rights and patient rights.**
    Ésta es información sobre sus derechos de privacidad y derechos del
    paciente.

25. **Who should we call to do it?**
    ¿A quién debemos llamar para hacerlo?

    Note: Literally "Whom we ought to call to do it?" A better
    translation would be: "¿A quién deberíamos llamar para
    hacerlo?"

26. **No, I don't know anyone.**
    No, no conozco a nadie.

    Note: "conozco" is present tense, the verb "conocer" is irregular.

27. Would you like me to call?
¿Quiere que yo llame?

> Notes: Literally means: "Would you like me to call?." 2. "Quiere", is simple present, "querer" is irregular.

28. Please, come this way.
¿Por favor, puede venir por aquí?

> Notes: 1. Literaly "Please, can you come by here." 2. The imperative tense (orders) may sound rude; using the presente tense in a question instead solves this.

29. I am going to measure it.
Lo voy a medir.

30. I am going to write the report to the project manager.
Voy a escribir el informe al director de proyectos.

31. I am going to write it to him.
Se lo voy a escribir.

32. I am going to take your pulse/ preassure.
Voy a tomarle el pulso/ la presión sanguínea.

33. Why is there a delay? Because there has been an accident.
¿Por qué hay un retraso? Porque ha habido un accidente.

34. I don't like the hotels near airports.
No me gustan los hoteles cerca de los aeropuertos.

> Note: The verb "gustar" is conjugated the reverse. *(Chapter 14 Translating "It Appeals to me")*.
>
> Me duele is literally "It hurts." The verb "doler" is irregular, and of the family of "gustar" *(Chapter 14 Translating "It Appeals to me")*.

35. My stomach hurts.
Me duele el estómago.

> Note. Me duele is literally "It hurts." The verb "doler" is irregular, and of the family of "gustar" *(Chapter 14 Translating "It Appeals to me")*.

36. **What happened?**
¿Qué pasó?

37. **How long has the work been stopped?**
¿Cuánto tiempo llevan los trabajos parados?

38. **Since Tuesday. For two days.**
Desde el martes. Dos días.

39. **It takes three days to move the offices to the new location.**
Lleva tres dias hacer la mudanza de las oficinas al nuevo lugar.

40. **What requirements do we have to meet?**
¿Qué requisitos tenemos que cumplir?

        Note: Or more formally ¿Qué requisitos tenemos que satisfacer?

41. **Have you met the new director?**
¿Has conocido al nuevo director?

42. **Do you know the new director?**
¿Conoces al nuevo director?

43. **Do you know anything about purchasing?**
¿Sabes algo sobre (gestión de) compras?

        Note: The translation of "to meet" and to "know" as
        "conocer" and "saber", depends on the context.

44. **How often you do have a briefing with you client?**
¿Con qué frecuencia tienes una reunión de informe con tu cliente?

45. **The client will ask you for a debrief on the accident at the site?**
El cliente te va a pedir una reunion para preguntas sobre el accidente
en la obra.

46. **I write a cost report every two weekks**
Escribo un informe cada dos semanas

47. **[(2+3)x4]/5**
Dos más tres, por cuatro, entre cinco.

48. $2^4=16$
Dos elevado a cuatro es dieciséis

49. $\sin(180°) = \pi$
El seno de 90 es pi

50. How many languages do you speak?
¿Cuántos idiomas hablas?

51. Ana's car is broken.
El carro de Ana está roto.

52. Where is Coca Cola factory?
¿Dónde está la fabrica de Coca Cola?

53. There must be a smoke detector in each bedroom.
Tiene que haber un detector de humos en cada dormitorio.

> Note: 1. In Spanish nouns functioning as adjectives (smoke), go after the actual noun with the preposition "de," detector de humos (detector of smoke).

54. I believe the calculations are not correct.
Creo que los cálculos no son correctos.

> Note: Unlike English, the word "que" maynot be omitted in this kind of sentences.

55. How is the request for quotation in this company?
¿Cómo es el proceso de salir a oferta en tu compañía?

56. When did it start?
¿Cuándo ha comenzado?

57. I can send it by email.
Puedo enviarlo por *email*.

> Note: Words that come from the new technologies tend to be used as in the original language. In the case of *email*, there's another term in Spanish "correo electrónico;" but *email* is very used and is even included in the dictionary Real Academia Español. Remember that a Spanish word that come from other

language as is, and with different rules of pronounciation, needs
be writen in *italics*. This is also the case of words as marketing
(mercadotecnia). *(*See the Technical vocabulary of *Chapter 1
The Alphabet*).

58. I have to check the driver of the program.
Tengo que chequear el *driver* del programa.

> Note: "Chequear" is an adaptation of "to check" and it is in the
> dictionary. 2. Other words, as *driver*, haven't been included in
> the Spanish dictionary (yet).

59. We work with IBM in this project
Estamos trabajando con IBM en este proyecto (I.B.M. i-be-eme)

> Note: 1. Literally "We are working with IBM in this project."
> 2. Acronyms are pronounced either letter by letter, as IBM, or as
> a whole word "RENFE" /renfe/ Red Nacional de Ferrocarriles
> Españoles.

**60. Water is the component you need to mix with quicklime to
obtain slack lime, lime for construction use.**
El agua es el componente que necesitas mezclar con la cal viva para
obtener cal apagada, la cal para uso en la construcción.

> Note: 1. The article to use with the word "agua" is "el". This is to
> avoid the bad sound of " la agua." This happens when the noun
> in question starts with an stressed "a." However "agua" is a
> feminine word: agua sucia (not "agua sucio"), dirty water. 2.
> Unlike English, the word "que" maynot be omitted in this kind of
> sentences.

61. The cost depends on the materials.
El coste depende de los materiales.
> Note: 1. The prepotions (as "de") that follow the verbs in Spanish
> and English maynot coincide: "depende de" (not "depende en").

62. We are going to resume the welding. Put your mask back on.
Vamos a retomar la soldadura. Te debes poner la máscara otra vez.

> Note: 1. Unlike English, Spanish verbs never have a proposition
> after, as a part of it, as "to put on" (poner). 2. The translation of
> "back" is commonly "otra vez" (again).

63. I'll come back to the office on wednesday.
Voy a volver a la oficina el miércoles.

> Note: Here the verb "come back" (a verb with preposition) is translated for "volver" (to return).

64. I hope the specialist can come today.
Espero que el especialista pueda venir hoy.

> Note: 1. The tense of the verb "poder" here is the present subjunctive. This is an extra present tense in Spanish. It is only used in some subjective cases when you have more than one clause, here I hope, and The specialist come today. 2. Unlike English, the word "que" maynot be omitted in this kind of sentences.

65. Welding can be dangerous.
Soldar puede ser peligroso.

> Note: The word "welding" comes from a verb (to weld) but it functions here as a noun. In general, the English form of the verb that works as a noun s the "ing" word (the gerund), whereas the Spanish form of the verb that works as a noun is the infinitive (ar, er, ir forms).

66. The U.S. is very dependand on foreign oil.
EE.UU. (Estados Unidos) es muy dependiente del petróleo extranjero.

> Note: In English "oil" is an abreviation of "crude oil" from petroleum. In Spanish the term used is "crudo" or more commonly "petróleo". "Aceite" (oil) is a generic term for all low density products that don't mix with water and are used as lubricants, e.g. "aceite de oliva" (olive oil). The context is what givess the exact meaning of the word in these cases.

> Another example is the term architect, which may mean "arquitecto" (a longer bachelor program), or "aparejador."

67. The height of the attic will be one meter greater.
La altura del ático será un metro mayor.

> Note: This is the opposite case of the previous sentence. Here we have two English words (attic and penthouse) that give the same translation into Spanish, "ático." The term "'ático" is generic for the last floor of a building, regardless of its use, a service area or a luxurios apartment, penthouse.

Other examples are: roof ("cubierta") and ceiling ("techo"), which are both commonly translated by "techo;" or chimney and fireplace, both "chimenea;" or dust and powder, both "polvo."

68. The brindge will be made of concrete.
El puente va a estar hecho de concreto.

Note: In Spain, they use the word "hormigón, instead of "concreto." We find many examples of technical concepts that use different tems in different dialects in English, as "skirting board" in UK and baseboard in the US ("rodapiés" in Spanish).

Other examples are: civil engineer, "ingeniero de caminos" in Spain (ingeniero de caminos, canales y puertos), and "ingeniero civil" in Latin America; or "bombilla," light bulb in Spain, or "foco" in Mexico.

69. I have a pain in my arm.
Tengo un dolor en el brazo.

Note: 1.Literally I have a pain in the arm. Spanish use the article "el/la/los/las instead of the posessive (mi/tu/su, etc.). when the subject is obvious.

70. That electric panel will be connected directly to the main.
Ese cuadro eléctrico va a estar conectado directamente a la acometida eléctrica.

Note: The term "acometida", as the English "main" refers to the main line (electric, gas, water, etc.) where the services to a building come from.

71. The load will be 100 kW
La carga será de cien kilovatios.

Note: "Carga, "as load" is a generic concept with easy transferable meaning to different disciplines: thermal load, structural load, preassure demanded from a pump, etc.

72. This project is broken down into three phases.
El proyecto está desglosado en tres fases.

Note: Past participles ("desglosado") go commonly with the verb "estar" (versus "ser") since they define a state. (see the technical vocabulary of *Chapter 17 Next Steps in Spanish*).

73. **Is it automatic?**
    ¿Es automático?

> Note: 1. Technical adjectives (automático) go commonly with the verb "ser" (versus "estar") since they define a inherent attribute of the noun. (See the Technical Vocabulary of *Chapter 17 Next Steps in Spanish*). 2. The word "it" when working as a pronoun (this is, in the begining of a sentence) is ommited in Spanish.

74. **It's cold outside but the the building is hot and I am hot.**
    Hace frío fuera pero el edificio está caliente y yo tengo calor.

> Note: The translation of "to be" may be "ser," "estar," "tener," or "hacer" (see the General Vocabulary of *Chapter 8 How to learn words Efficiently*).

75. **In this building internal walls are made up of bricks.**
    En este edificio las paredes están hechas de fábrica de ladrillo.

> Note: "Fábrica de ladrillo" indicates the building is made using brinks as the main component . In the same way, "fábrica de bloques de cemento" is a construction out of cement blocks.

APPENDICES

APPENDIX A

NOTES ABOUT DIALECTS
NOTAS SOBRE DIALECTOS

APPENDIX A: NOTES ABOUT DIALECTS
NOTAS SOBRE DIALECTOS

All languages have dialects. In the same way that English speakers from United Kingdom, Ireland, United States or Australia speak the same language differently; speakers from Spain, Argentina or Mexico have recognizable differences.

Nonetheless, Spanish is a very unified language. The rules of grammar and spelling are the same all over the Spanish-speaking world. The differences between dialects are limited mostly to the preference of some words over others, and some differences in the pronunciation.

English	Example 1	Example 2
US English	line	tomato /tomeito/
UK English	queue	tomato /tomatoh/

Spanish		
Mexican Spanish	fila (= line)	jitomate (= tomato)
Spanish from Spain	cola	tomate

The Spanish spoken in the southwest of United States (mostly California, Arizona, Texas and New Mexico) belongs for the most part, to the realm of the Mexican dialect. In addition, the Spanish in the US is, of course, influenced by the English language, and some words used are not part of the standard.

	Example 1	Example 2	Example 3
English	market	carpet	truck
Non-standard Spanish	marketa	carpeta	troca
Spanish	mercado	alfombra	camión

A language can be divided into dialects and, in turn, those dialects can be subdivided into subdialects indefinitely. However, we can consider three main dialects with the following representatives:

- the Spanish from Spain
- the Spanish from Latin America except Argentina
- the Spanish from Argentina

The most apparent difference among the dialects in Spanish is the use of the pronouns and the verb forms thereof, as shown in the following table:

	Spain	Latin America	Argentina
I sing	(yo) canto	← THE SAME	← THE SAME
You (singular) sing	**(tú) cantas**	← THE SAME	**(vos) cantás ***
He/ She sings	(él /ella) canta	← THE SAME	← THE SAME
We sing	(nosotros) cantamos	← THE SAME	← THE SAME
You guys sing	**(vosotros) cantáis**	**(ustedes) cantan**	← THE SAME
They sing	(ellos) cantan	← THE SAME	← THE SAME

* Notice that the stress is on the last "a."

When addressing someone **formally**, the pronouns used are the same in all three dialects:

	Spain	Latin America	Argentina
sir/ ma'am, you sing	(usted) canta	← THE SAME	← THE SAME
sirs/ ma'ams, you sing	(ustedes) cantan	← THE SAME	← THE SAME

Thus, only in Spain there is a distinction for the plural form "you:" *vosotros* (informal), *ustedes* (formal).

Spanish from Spain

Except in the Southern area, Spain uses the English *th* **sound** for both the letter **z**, and the letter **c** when combined in **ce**, **ci** (as is explained in this book).

In Spain, they use **vosotros** (= you guys). "Vosotros" is one form taught in this book. In Spain, they also use "usted" (= you singular) and "ustedes" (= you plural), but only either to mark a distance from the person you are addressing, like addressing a stranger, or to show respect, like addressing a professor.

Usted uses the forms of "él/ella," e.g. "Usted estudia mucho." In the same way, "ustedes" uses the forms of "ellos," e.g. "Ustedes estudian mucho."

Only in Spain it is used the forms of the second person of plural, and its pronouns, which are:

> **"vosotros"** (or vosotras) as in **"vosotros cantáis"** (= you guys study). In Latin America: **"ustedes cantan."**

> **"vuestro"** (or "vuestra," "vuestros," "vuestras") as in "vuestro amigo" (= the friend of you guys). In Latin America: **"Su** amigo."

> **"os"** as in "Os veo" (= I see you guys). In Latin America: **"Los** veo."

A rule to use the forms of **vosotros** is simply to substitute the ending "mos" of **nosotros** for "is." Thus,

> Nosotros cant**amos** → Vosotros cant**áis**
> Nosotros beb**emos** → Vosotros beb**éis**
> Nosotros viv**ímos** → Vosotros viv**ís**

> (= We sing, drink, live -- You guys sing, drink, live)

This rule works for most of the irregular verbs too, e.g. dormir (= to sleep)

> Nosotros dorm**imos** → Vosotros dorm**ís**

There are three exceptions:

a) The verb "haber" (= to have)

> Nosotros he**mos** estudiado → Vosotros hab**éis** estudiado
> (no: Vosotros ~~heis~~ estudiado)

(= We have studied -- You guys have studied)

b) The nosotros form when ending in "imos". In this case, the vosotros form will have only one "I," e.g. :

> Nosotros vivi**mos** → Vosotros viv**ís**
> (not: Vosotros ~~viviis~~)

(= We live -- You guys live)

c) The past tense. For this tense, the vosotros form can be created out of the "tú" form just by adding "is," e.g.:

> Tú cantaste → Vosotros cantaste**is**
> Tú bebiste → Vosotros bebiste**is**
> Tú vivíste → Vosotros viviste**is**

Spanish from Latin America

In Latin America, they use the **/s/ sound** for the letter **c** when combined in **ce, ci,** and the letter **z** (instead of the /th/ sound used in Spain). So, they don't distinguish between "caza" (= hunting) and "casa" (= house), or between "coser" (= to sew) and "cocer"(= to boil).

Latin America **never uses "vosotros."** Instead, "ustedes" is used. Remember: **ustedes** uses the same forms of "ellos" e.g. Ustedes <u>estudian</u> mucho y ellos <u>estudian</u> poco (= You guys study a lot, but they study little).

In some areas of Latin American, they never use "tú." They use "usted" instead. Remember: "usted" uses the same forms of "él/ella" e.g. Usted <u>estudia</u> mucho y él <u>estudia</u> poco (= You study a lot, but he studies little).

Spanish from Argentina

In regards to the characteristics of Spanish spoken in Latin America, Argentina shows two specific differences: the use of **"vos,"** and the pronunciation of the **strong "ll."**

Argentina has a very strong pronunciation of both the "ll," and the "y" as a consonant. It sounds close to the English "g" in George or the "sh" in shoe, depending on the speaker.

Argentina uses vos (= you singular) instead of "tú." Generally speaking, "vos" goes with the forms of "vosotros" but eliminates the -i- of the last syllable. Example:

vosotros cantáis → vos cantás.

This rule only applies for the simple present (vos cantás).

The commands –a tense not studied in this book- also makes a transformation from the original "vosotros." It uses the form of vosotros but eliminates the final "d."

Cantad vosotros → cantá vos

Vos, for the rest of the tenses follow the standard rules of conjugation of "tú."

"Vos" does not have its own set of associated pronouns, so it uses the ones of "tú." Examples:

Vos, a **tu** manera… (= you, in your way, …).
A vos **te** canta María (= Maria sings to you).
No tenés que ir**te** (= You don't have to go).

The use of vos is called "voseo." Argentina is where voseo is norm. Uruguay, Paraguay and other areas of Latin America use "vos," but their rules are not consistent, as those in Argentina, and it is not considered standard.

APPENDIX B

NOTES ABOUT CULTURE
NOTAS SOBRE CULTURA

APPENDIX B: NOTES ABOUT CULTURE
NOTAS SOBRE CULTURA

In the process of communicating some knowledge about the culture of the speaker can be crucial. Below are some features that may be distinctive of the culture in the Spanish speaking countries.

1. Figures

Remember that the Spanish word **billón** doesn't mean *billion*. Instead, one **billón** equals 1000 billions.

> 1,000,000,000 is one billion.
> 1,000,000,000 es mil millones.
>
> 1,000,000,000,000 is one thousand billion.
> 1,000,000,000,000 es un billón.

Spanish never expresses figures neither in tens nor in hundreds.

> 1900 is nineteen hundred.
> 1900 es mil novecientos.
>
> 1995 is nineteen, ninety five.
> 1995 es mil novecientos noventa y cinco

Unlike English, in Spanish the comma is frequently used to indicate decimal and the period is used to indicate thousands.

> Pi is 3.14 approximately.
> Pi es 3,14 aproximadamente.

2,000 is two thousand.
2.000 es dos mil.

In Spanish, monetary figures have the symbol of the currency at the end.

2.000,50 $ son dos mil dólares con cincuenta centavos.
$2,000.50 is two thousand dollars and fifty cents.

2. Units of measurement

Remember that many countries only use units of measurement of the International System (also called metric system, or decimal system).

Below is a table with the names of the basic units, their abbreviations, and their conversion to U.S. system units.

Abrev.	Spanish	English	Conversion
g	gramo	gram	1 g = 0.03 oz (onzas de peso)
Kg	kilo	kilo	1 Kg = 2.2 Lb (libras)
m	metro	meter	1 m =3.28 ft (pies)
cm	centímetro	centimeter	1 cm =0.39 inch (pulgadas)
Km	kilómetro	kilometer	1 Km = 0.62 miles (millas)
l	litro	liter	1 l = 0.26 gal (galones) 1 l = 33.81 fl oz (onzas de líquido)
°C	Celsius	Celsius	37 C = 98.6 °F (Fahrenheit) *

(*) The conversion from Celsius to Fahrenheit is not linear. The formulae is: °F = (°C x 9/5) + 32. The range 37 C to 39 C, of the table, corresponds to common fever.

3. Dates

Dates are given in this order: day, month, and year:

01/31/12 is January thirty first, two thousand twelve.
31/01/12 es el treinta y uno de enero de dos mil doce.

Years, as any figure, are **never** expressed in tens or hundreds. (See "Figures" above).

In Spanish calendars, the week starts on Monday –not on Sunday.

4. Tú vs. Usted

In those regions where both **tú** and **usted** are used (some regions only use usted), "tú" is used to address someone informally, and "usted" formally.

Every Spanish-speaking country has its different social codes, and they accept "tú" in different levels of familiarity. This is why it is recommended that you use "usted" always, unless the patient addresses you differently.

Usted is abbreviated as Ud. or Vd.; and **ustedes,** as Uds. or Vds.

5. Courtesy

Use **por favor** (= please) extensively. It could sound rude otherwise, specially with commands.

> Por favor, puedes venir por aquí (not: Ven por aquí).
> Please, can you come this way.

Smiling and using the courtesy tags will really help you gain your patient's confidence and respect.

> Gracias. De nada. Por favor. Lo siento
> Thank you. You're welcome. Please. I am sorry.

6. The two last names

In many Spanish speaking countries the naming system includes the father's and mother's paternal family names.

The first name, **el nombre** or **el nombre de pila** (= the Baptism name) can be one or more names, i.e. José Carlos, Marco Antonio.

The first surname, **el apellido**, or **el primer apellido**, or **el apellido del padre** (= the father's surname) is always the person's father's last name.

The second surname, **el segundo apellido**, or **el apellido de la madre** (= the mother's surname) is the person mother's last name.

For example, Antonio Álvarez Ala and Beatriz Barroso Barrio's have a child. They name him Luis. Consequently, Luis' full name is: Luis Álvarez Barroso.

7. The Pace of the Day

The stages of the day are: **la mañana**, which lasts from the sunrise until lunch time (at 1, 2 or even 3 pm); **la tarde**, until sunset; and **la noche**, when it's dark. So, Spanish doesn't distinguish between afternoon and evening. They both are **la tarde**.

The strongest meal of the day is commonly **la comida** or **el almuerzo** (= lunch). **El desayuno** and **la cena** (= breakfast and dinner) are lighter meals. All these meals are typically taken later than their counterparts in the English culture. In addition, people may have a snack before lunch, called **el aperitivo,** or before dinner, called **la merienda**.

Traditionally, people have a nap, **la siesta**, after lunch. It is believed that this tradition is a result of having a heavy meal and high temperatures at the time of that meal. One common characteristic of the Spanish-speaking countries is the hot climate. Spain enjoys hot summers; so does her sister countries in the Americas. Even Argentina and Chile, with extreme latitude, have regions with hot summers.
Nowadays, work schedules with long commutes and short lunch breaks don't allow time for this nap; however, in summertime and during holidays many people in those countries have a nap after lunch.

8. Greetings

The formal manner to greet is with a handshake.

Among family and friends, it is extended in the Spanish-speaking world to give one **beso** (= kiss) or two on the cheeks as a way of greeting. The kiss exchange occurs woman-woman or man-woman.

APPENDIX C

PRESENT TENSE
EL PRESENTE DE INDICATIVO

APPENDIX C: PRESENT TENSE
EL PRESENTE DE INDICATIVO

Regular Verbs

	AR Verbs	ER Verbs	IR Verbs
(I)	-o	-o	-o
(you singular)	-as	-es	-es
(he/she/it)	-a	-e	-e
(we)	-amos	-emos	-imos
(you guys)- Spain-	-ais	-eis	-ís
(you guys/ they)	-an	-en	-en

	cantar	beber	partir
(I)	canto	bebo	parto
(you singular)	cantas	bebes	partes
(he/she/it)	canta	bebe	parte
(we)	cantamos	bebemos	partimos
(you guys)- Spain-	cantáis	bebéis	partís
(you guys/ they)	cantan	beben	parten

We marked the persons in parentheses to denote that in Spanish, it is redundant to put it because the information on who did the action is already in the ending. You don't need to say "Yo canto" (I sing), but just "Canto."

Examples of use of the present tense:

    I sing, you sing, he sings, we sing, you guys sing, they sing
    Canto, cantas, canta, cantamos, cantáis, cantan

    I drink, you drink, he drinks, we drink, you guys drink, they drink
    Bebo, bebes, bebe, bebemos, bebéis, beben

    I live, you live, he lives, we live, you guys live, they live
    Vivo, vives, vive, vivimos, vivís, viven

Unlike English, in Spanish you can use the present tense to describe historical facts.

    Columbus discovered America in 1492.
    Colón descubre America en 1492.

Spelling-changing or False-irregular Verbs

It may happen that the verb needs to alter its spelling to accommodate the right pronunciation. An example is **vencer** (= to defeat). If we add the endings to form the present tense, we obtain a wrong pronunciation of its forms. Venc-er /benthér/ → it should sound /benth-o/, but ~~venco~~ gives /benko/ instead.

	vencer
(I)	venzo
(you singular)	vences
(he/she/it)	vence
(we)	vencemos
(you guys)	vencéis
(they)	vencen

If you take the stem venc- and then add the suffix -o, the result is venco, but the "c" with "o" doesn't sound as "s" of vencer. That's why the spelling needs to change.

This happens with the verbs ending in:

-cer → -zo
-cir → -zo
-ger → -jo
-gir → -jo
-guir → -go
-quir → -co

Warning

You don't have to memorize these endings. As you learn the rules of spelling of this book, you will notice when you write them (remember: pronunciation wise, they are regular). Notice that it is the same transformation of:
poco (= little of) + ito → poquito (= little bit of), not ~~pocito~~

Examples:

	-cer → -zo	**-cir → -zo**	**-ger → -jo**
	vencer	esparcir	proteger
	= to defeat	= to spread	= to protect
(I)	venzo	esparzo	protejo
(you singular)	vences	esparces	proteges
(he/she/it)	vence	esparce	protege
(we)	vencemos	esparcimos	protegemos
(you guys)-Sp.	vencéis	esparcís	protegéis
(you guys/ they)	vencen	esparcen	protegen

	-gir → jo	**-guir → -go**	**quie → -co**
	exigir	distinguir	delinquir
	= to demand	= to distinguish	= to commit a crime
(I)	exijo	distingo	delinco
(you singular)	exiges	distingues	delinques
(he/she/it)	exige	distingue	delinque
(we)	exigimos	distinguimos	delinquimos
(you guys)-Sp.	exigís	distinguís	delinquís
(you guys/ they)	exigent	distinguen	delinquen

All these verbs are the spelling-changing verbs. Those that happen to be regular can also be called false-irregular verbs.

Also notice that these alterations can also happen when the verb is irregular for other reasons. For example "seguir" (= to follow) is truly irregular (not what we called "false irregular"). As it is explained in the following Corollary, Type 4, with the verb "**seguir**" forms "**sigo**" (I follow). So, it changes its stem; it is irregular. It is in addition to that, that it needs to alter its "u" to accommodate to the right pronunciation, according to the above rules ("sigo," not ~~siguo~~).

These alterations only take place with the Present tense, Preterite (*Chapter 23 Preterite*) and Present Subjunctive (*Chapter 28 Present Subjunctive*).

The Irregular Verbs in the Present Tense

There are six types of irregularities:

Type 1 Affects all verbs ending in –uir

> These verbs add "**y**" after the stem to form present tense, except for the forms nosotros and vosotros.

> Example: construir (= to construct) construo → construyo

(I)	construyo
(you singular)	construyes
(he/she/it)	construye
(we)	construimos
(you guys) -Spain	construís
(you guys/ they)	construyen

Shading indicates irregularity

The rule of the slipper. Some Californian teachers use the term "la regla de la zapatilla" based on the shape that results when you display the conjugation in two columns:

construyo	construimos
construyes	construís
construye	construyen

Other examples are: atribuir, contribuir, distribuir (= to attribute, to contribute, to distribute).

Type 2. Affects most verbs with an -o- in the second to last syllable.

These verbs change -o- → -ue- , except for the forms nosotros and vosotros, to form present tense.

Example: dor-mir (= to sleep)

(I)	**duermo**
(you singular)	**duermes**
(he/she/it)	**duerme**
(we)	dormimos
(you guys) –Spain-	dormís
(you guys/ they)	**duermen**

Shading indicates irregularity

Notice the "rule of the slipper" explained above.

Other examples are: poder, morir, mover, contar (= can, to die, to move, to count).

Nonetheless, there are verbs like "co-mer," or "co-ser" (= to eat, to sew) which are regular.

Type 3. Affects most verbs with an –e- in the second to last syllable.

Some of these verbs change –e- → -ie- , except for the forms nosotros and vosotros. **Other verbs** of this type change according to the **type 4**.

Example: pre-fe-rir (= to prefer)

(I)	prefiero
(you singular)	prefieres
(he/she/it)	prefiere
(we)	preferimos
(you guys) –Spain-	preferís
(you guys/ they)	prefieren

Shading indicates irregularity

Notice that we have here the "rule of the slipper" explained above.

Other examples are: entender, querer, sentir (= to understand, to want, to feel).

Nonetheless, there are verbs like "be-ber" or "pesar" (= to drink, to weigh) which are regular.

Type 4. Affects most verbs with an –e- in the second to last syllable.

Some of these verbs change –e- → -i- , except for the forms nosotros and vosotros. Other verbs of this type change according to the previous type.

Example: re-pe-tir (= to repeat)

(I)	repito
(you singular)	repites
(he/she/it)	repite
(we)	repetimos
(you guys) –Spain-	repetís
(you guys/ they)	repiten

Shading indicates irregularity

Notice that we have here the "rule of the slipper" explained above.
Other examples are: seguir, conseguir, pedir (= to follow, to achieve, to ask for).

So, a verb with an –e- in the second to last syllable can be irregular ie-irregular i-irregular or regular (preferir, repetir, pensar).

Nonetheless, notice that, as in the previous type, there are verbs like "be-ber" or "pesar" (= to drink, to weigh) which are regular.

Type 5. Affects most verbs ending with –cer or –cir , except "decir."

These verbs add "z" before the "c," for the form "I." Example:

producir (= to produce)

(I)	produzco
(you singular)	produces
(he/she/it)	produce
(we)	producimos
(you guys) –Spain-	producís
(you guys/ they)	producen

Shading indicates irregularity

Other examples are: conocer, conducir, crecer, (= to know, to drive, to grow up).

Nonetheless, there are verbs as "vencer" or "convencer" (= to defeat, to convince) which are regular.

Type 6. Others.

There are **21 verbs** which don't follow any rule. However they can be grouped by their similar changes.

12 verbs end with "–go" for the form of "I" (instead of "-o").

These are:

tener, venir, decir, bendecir, hacer, satisfacer, valer, traer, poner, salir, caer, oír.
(to have, to come, to say, to bless, to do, to satisfy, to be worth, to bring, to put, to go out, to fall, to hear)

	tener	**venir**
(I)	tengo	vengo
(you singular)	tienes	vienes
(he/she/it)	tiene	viene
(we)	tenemos	venimos
(you guys) –Spain-	tenéis	venís
(you guys/ they)	tienen	vienen

	decir	**bendecir ***
(I)	digo	bendigo
(you singular)	dices	bendices
(he/she/it)	dice	bendice
(we)	decimos	bendecimos
(you guys) –Spain-	decís	bendecís
(you guys/ they)	dicen	bendicen

	hacer	**satisfacer ***
(I)	hago	satisfago
(you singular)	haces	satisfaces
(he/she/it)	hace	satisface
(we)	hacemos	satisfacemos
(you guys) –Spain-	hacéis	satisfacéis ·
(you guys/ they)	hacen	satisfacen

	traer	**valer**	**poner**
(I)	traigo	valgo	pongo
(you singular)	traes	vales	pones
(he/she/it)	trae	vale	pone
(we)	traemos	valemos	ponemos
(you guys) –Spain-	traéis	valéis	ponéis
(you guys/ they)	traen	valen	ponen

Shading indicates irregularity

	salir	caer	oír
(I)	salgo	caigo	oigo
(you singular)	sales	caes	oyes
(he/she/it)	sale	cae	oye
(we)	salimos	caemos	oímos
(you guys) –Spain-	salís	caéis	oís
(you guys/ they)	salen	caen	oyen

(*) The rules are also applicable to all verbs that derive from them like "poner" and "suponer" (= to put and to suppose). However, although "satisfacer" and "bendecir" look like derivative verbs of hacer and decir respectively, they are not. You will see that they are not linked in other tenses.

Four verbs end with "–y" for the form of "I" (instead of "–o"). These are: dar, estar, ser, and ir (= to give, to be, to be, to go).

	dar	estar	ser	ir
(I)	doy	estoy	soy	voy
(you singular)	das	estás	eres	vas
(he/she/it)	da	está	es	va
(we)	damos	estamos	somos	vamos
(you guys) –Spain-	dais	estáis	sois	vais
(you guys/ they)	da	están	son	van

Five verbs don't have any specific ending. These are: saber, ver, caber, jugar, haber (= to know, to see, to fit, to play, to have –auxiliary).

	saber	ver	caber	jugar *	haber
(I)	sé	veo	quepo	juego	he
(you s.)	sabes	ves	cabes	juegas	has
(he/she/it)	sabe	ve	cabe	juega	ha
(we)	sabemos	vemos	cabemos	jugamos	hemos
(you guys) –Spain-	sabéis	veis	cabéis	jugáis	habéis
(you guys/ they)	saben	ven	caben	juegan	han

Shading indicates irregularity

(*) Notice that the verb "jugar" seems to fit into the type-2 irregularity (o → ue); however this verb does not have a "o," but an "u," in the second to last syllable.

Note about irregular verbs

Certain tenses share the same irregularities. You will see similar types of irregularities of the Present when you study the Present Subjunctive.

APPENDIX D

TABLE OF ENDINGS OF THE REGULAR VERBS
TABLA DE TERMINACIONES DE LOS VERBOS REGULARES

APPENDIX D: TABLE OF ENDINGS OF THE REGULAR VERBS

TABLA DE TERMINACIONES DE LOS VERBOS REGULARES

Impersonal Forms of the Verb

	AR verbs	ER verbs	IR verbs
Infinitive (to sing)	-ar	-er	-ir

	AR verbs	ER verbs	IR verbs
Gerund (singing)	-ando	-iendo	-iendo

	AR verbs	ER verbs	IR verbs
Past Participle (sung)	-ado	-ido	-ido

Personal Forms of the Verb: Indicative Mood

Present (I sing)	AR verbs	ER verbs	IR verbs
(I)	-o	-o	-o
(you singular)	-as	-es	-es
(he/she/it)	-a	-e	-e
(we)	-amos	-emos	-imos
(you guys) -Spain-	-ais	-éis	-ís
(you guys/ they)	-an	-en	-en

Preterite (I sang)	AR verbs	ER verbs	IR verbs
(I)	-é	-í	-í
(you singular)	-aste	-iste	-iste
(he/she/it)	-ó	-ió	-ió
(we)	-amos	-imos	-imos
(you guys) -Spain-	-asteis	-isteis	-isteis
(you guys/ they)	-aron	-ieron	-ieron

Imperfect Past (I sang*)	AR verbs	ER verbs	IR verbs
(I)	-aba	-ía	-ía
(you singular)	-abas	-ías	-ías
(he/she/it)	-aba	-ía	-ía
(we)	-ábamos	-íamos	-íamos
(you guys) -Spain-	-abais	-íais	-íais
(you guys/ they)	-aban	-ían	-ían

Future (I will sing)

	AR verbs	ER verbs	IR verbs
(I)	-aré	-eré	-iré
(you singular)	-arás	-erás	-irás
(he/she/it)	-ará	-erá	-irá
(we)	-aremos	-eremos	-iremos
(you guys) -Spain-	-aréis	-eréis	-iréis
(you guys/ they)	-arán	-erán	-irán

Conditional (I would sing)

	AR verbs	ER verbs	IR verbs
(I)	-aría	-ería	-iría
(you singular)	-arías	-erías	-irías
(he/she/it)	-aría	-ería	-iría
(we)	-aríamos	-eríamos	-iríamos
(you guys) -Spain-	-aríais	-eríais	-iríais
(you guys/ they)	-arían	-erían	-irían

Personal Forms of the Verb: Imperative Mood

Imperative (Sing!)

	AR verbs	ER verbs	IR verbs
(I)			
(you singular)	-a	-e	-e
(he/she/it)			
(we)			
(you guys) -Spain-	-ad	-ed	-id
(you guys/ they)			

Personal Forms of the Verb: Subjunctive Mood

Present (...that I sing)

	AR verbs	ER verbs	IR verbs
(I)	-e	-a	-a
(you singular)	-es	-as	-as
(he/she/it)	-e	-a	-a
(we)	-emos	-amos	-amos
(you guys) -Spain-	-éis	-áis	-áis
(you guys/ they)	-en	-an	-an

Past (...that I sang)

	AR verbs	ER verbs	IR verbs
(I)	-ara	-iera	-iera
(you singular)	-aras	-ieras	-ieras
(he/she/it)	-ara	-iera	-iera
(we)	-áramos	-iéramos	-iéramos
(you guys) -Spain-	-arais	-ierais	-ierais
(you guys/ they)	-aran	-ieran	-ieran

-or-

	AR verbs	ER verbs	IR verbs
(I)	-ase	-iese	-iese
(you singular)	-ases	-ieses	-ieses
(he/she/it)	-ase	-iese	-iese
(we)	-ásemos	-iésemos	-iésemos
(you guys) -Spain-	-aseis	-ieseis	-ieseis
(you guys/ they)	-asen	-iesen	-iesen

INDEX OF GRAMMATICAL WORDS

INDEX OF GRAMMATICAL WORDS
ÍNDICE DE PALABRAS GRAMATICALES

The following is a list of words with grammatical meaning as explained in *Chapter 11 Grammar Rules*. It gathers the words from the General Vocabulary sections of this .book

In the following table:

- Underscore indicates the point of stress. One vowel words or words with accent mark are not indicated.

- The ellipses (…) at the end of a term indicates that the word must be followed by a noun or an adjective, i.e. "any…" in "any patient can do it" vs "any" in "any can do it." The ellipses between two words indicates there is some content in between, e.g. "either or."

- A capitalized initial indicates the word or expression can function as a complete sentence, e.g. Hello.

- The last column gives a reference of the chapter where that word or that type of words are explained.

- Notice that no indication about the gender (masculine/ feminine) is needed: none of these words are nouns (nouns are not grammatical words)

English	Spanish	Chapter
a	un , una	6
a lot	mucho	6
a lot of...	mucho/a/os/as	6
according to	según	10
after	tras	10
against	contra	10
all	todo/a/os/as el/la/los/las...	6
although	aunque	10
and	y	10
another	otro/ a	6
any, whichever	cualquiera	6
any..., whichever	cualquier...	6
around...	alrededor de...	10
as	a medida que	10
as	como	10
as per	en cuanto a...	10
as soon as	tan pronto como	10
at	en, a	10
at/ in the beginning of...	al principio de...	10
at/ in the end of...	al final de	10
because	porque	10
because of	por	10
because of	por causa de	10
between, among	entre	10
both	los dos	6
but	pero	10
but	sino	10
by	por	10
due to	debido a	10
either...or...	o...o..	10
everything	todo	6
excuse me	Con permiso	4
far from	lejos de	10
for	para, por	10
from	desde, de	10
given that	dado que	10

English	Spanish	Chapter
Good afternoon	Buenas tardes	4
Good evening, night	Buenas noches	4
Good morning	Buenos días	4
Goodbye	Adiós	4
he	él	7
Hello	Hola	4
Help me!	¡Ayuda!	4
Help me!	¡Socorro!	4
her	su / sus	6
here	aquí, acá	5
hers	suyo /a / os / as	11
his (as in "his house")	su / sus	6
his (as in "This is his")	suyo /a / os / as	11
how (quest. & exclam.)	cómo	12
How long ago...?	¿Cuánto tiempo hace...?	12
How long...?	¿Por cuánto tiempo...?	12
How many...?	¿Cuánto/a/os/as...?	12
How much...?	¿Cuánto/a...?	12
How often...?	¿Con qué frecuencia...?	12
However	sin embargo	10
I	yo	7
I don't know.	No lo sé, No sé.	4
I wish!	Ojalá	4
I'm sorry	Perdón, Lo siento.	4
if	si	10
in	en	10
in case that	en el caso de que	10
in other words	en otras palabras	10
in spite of	a pesar de	10
in the middle of...	en medio de...	10
in view that	en vista de que, visto que	10
inside...	dentro de...	10
it	ello (to be omitted)	7
Its	su/ sus	6
Its	suyo /a / os / as	11
like	al igual que	10

English	Spanish	Chapter
like	como	10
little (amount)	poco	6
little (amount)…	poco/a …	6
Maybe	Tal vez, Quizá(s)	4
Me neither	Yo tampoco	4
Me too	Yo también	4
me	me, mí	11
mine	mío/ a/ os/ as	11
much	mucho / mucha	6
much	muchos/as	6
my	mi / mis	6
near, close to, around…	cerca de…	10
neither …nor…	ni…ni…	10
never	nunca , jamás	12
nevertheless	no obstante	10
next to…	junto a…	10
no	no	12
no…	ningún /ninguna	6
none	ninguno / ninguna	6
none of…	ninguno/a de …	6
nt	no	12
nthing	nada	6
now	ahora	5
of the	del = de el	6
of you guys	su, vuestro/a/os/as (Sp.)	7
of, from, off	de	10
Okay	Okey	4
on	sobre, en	10
on top of…	encima de…	10
or	o	10
other, others	otro/ a/ os /as	6
our, ours	nuestro/ a / os/ as	7
outside…	fuera de…	10
Please	Por favor	4
Really?	¿De verdad?	4
Right?	¿Verdad?	4

English	Spanish	Chapter
See you later	Hasta la vista	4
See you later	Hasta luego	4
See you soon	Hasta pronto	4
she	ella	7
side by side...	al lado de	10
since	puesto que, ya que	10
so that	para que	10
some	alguno /alguna	6
some of ...	alguno/a/os/as de...	6
some...	algún /a /os/ as, unos, unas	6
something	algo	6
supposing that	suponiendo que	10
Thank you	Gracias	4
Thank you very much	Muchas Gracias	4
that	aquel, aquella,aquello	6
that	ese/a, eso	6
the	el, la, los, las	6
their	su / sus	6
theirs	suyo /a / os / as	11
then, afterwards	entonces, luego	10
there	ahí, allí, allá	5
these	éstos/as	6
they	ellos	7
this	este/a, esto	6
those	ésos/as	6
those (farther)	aquellos/as	6
to	para, a	10
to herself	le, la, se	11
to herself	se	11
to him	le, lo, se	11
to himself	se	11
to it	le, la, lo, se	11
to itself	se	11
to me, to myself	me	11
to the, at the	al = a el	6
to themselves	se	11

English	Spanish	Chapter
to us, to ourselves	nos	11
to you (plural)	les, se	11
to you, to yourself	te	11
to you guys, yourselves	os (Spain)	11
to, at	a	10
to, towards	hacia	10
today	hoy	5
tomorrow	mañana	5
under...	bajo...	10
underneath	debajo de / abajo de	10
unless	a menos que	10
until, up to	hasta	10
we	nosotros	7
what	que	12
what (quest. & exclam.)	qué	12
when	cuando, cuándo	12
where	donde, dónde	12
which (in other cases)	cual/cuales, cuál/cuáles	12
while, as long as	mientras	10
who	quien/quienes, quién/quiénes	12
with	con	10
with me	conmigo	11
with you (informal)	contigo	11
without	sin	10
yes	sí	12
yesterday	ayer	5
you (obj. pronoun)	te, ti	11
you (singular)	tú	7
you guys	ustedes	7
you guys	vosotros (Spain)	7
You're welcome	De nada	4
your	su / sus (informal)	6
your	tu / tus (singular)	6
yours	suyo /a /os /as (de usted)	11
yours	tuyo/ a / os /as (de ti)	11

INDEX OF TECHNICAL WORDS

INDEX OF TECHNICAL WORDS
ÍNDICE DE PALABRAS TÉCNICAS

The following is a list of the words from the Technical Vocabulary sections of this book

In the following table:

- Underscore indicates the point of stress. One vowel words or words with accent mark are not indicated.

- The last column gives a reference of the chapter where that word is used.

- All words are nouns with the exception of those of chapter 17, which are all adjectives. The gender of the nouns (masculine/ feminine) are indicated only if the word doesn't end in "o" or "a."

English	Spanish	Chapter
angle	ángulo	15
anode	ánodo	8
anode	ánodo	9
antenna	antena	9
aparent power	potencia aparente	8
apartment building	edificio de apartamentos	5
apartment, flat	apartamento, piso	5
application	(la) aplicación	10
application	(la) aplicación	13
appraisal	(la) tasación	14
approximation	(la) aproximación	15
aqueduct	acueducto	5
arc	arco	6
arc	arco	15
arccosecant	(la) arcocosecante	15
arccosine	(el) arcocoseno	15
arccotangent	(el) arcotangente	15
arcsecant	(la) arcosecante	15
arcsine	arcoseno	15
arctangent	(la) arcotangente	15
area	(el) área	5
area	(el) área	15
arithmetic	aritmética	15
artificial	artificial	17
asistote	asístota	15
asset	activo	14
at sign (@)	arroba	10
atmosphere	atmósfera	2
attic, penthouse	ático	5
automatic	automático	17
average	media	15
Avogadro Number	número de Avogadro	11
axis	(el) eje	12
axis	(el) eje	15
back yard	patio de atrás	5

English	Spanish	Chapter
backup	copia de seguridad	10
bag	bolso	16
ball	bola	12
ball and socket joint	rótula	12
bandwidth	ancho de banda	9
bank	banco	14
bar	barra	12
bar	(el) bar	16
base	(la) base	7
base	(la) base	9
base	(la) base	15
baseboard, skirting board	(el) rodapié	6
basement	sótano	5
bathroom	baño, cuarto de baño	5
battery	batería	8
beam	viga	6
bearing	rodamiento	12
bed	cama	16
bedroom	dormitorio, recámara	5
benefit	beneficio	14
bill	factura	14
binder	carpeta	16
binder	(el) conglomerante	7
bit	(el) bit	9
black	negro	17
blade	el) álabe, pala	12
blockwork	fábrica de bloques	7
blog	(el) blog	16
blue	azul	17
blueprint, drawing	plano	13
board	mesa directiva	13
bolt	tornillo de tuerca	12
Boltzmann constant	constante de Boltzmann	11
bonus	bono	14
book	libro	16

English	Spanish	Chapter
boots	(las) botas	11
box office	ventanilla, taquilla	16
brake	freno	12
branch	sucursal	16
breadboard	placa de pruebas	9
breakdown	(el) desglose	13
breakfast	desayuno	16
brick	ladrillo	7
brickwork pillar	(el) machón, (el) pilar de fábrica	6
bridge	(el) puente	5
briefcase	(el) maletín	16
brown	marrón	17
budget	presupuesto	14
building	edificio	5
building	edificio	16
burner	(el) quemador	11
bus	(el) autobús	16
business card	tarjeta	16
business plan	(el) plan de negocio	14
bypass	(el) baipás	11
byte	(el) byte	2
C language	C (ce)	10
C++	C++ (ce más más)	10
cabinet	armario	16
cable	(el) cable	8
cable	(el) cable (de acero)	12
cable tray	bandeja	8
CAD	CAD (cad)	10
cafeteria	cafetería	16
calcite	calcita	7
calculation	cálculo	15
calculus	cálculo	15
calendar	calendario	16
call	llamada	13
calorie	caloría	2

English	Spanish	Chapter
cam	leva	12
camera	cámara	10
camera	cámara	16
campus	(el) campus	13
capacitance	(la) capacidad	8
capacitor	(el) condensador	8
capital	(el) capital	14
car	carro, (el) coche	16
carbon dioxide CO2	CO_2 dióxido de carbono	7
carbon monoxide CO	CO monóxido de carbono	7
card	tarjeta	10
carpentry	carpintería	7
carpet	moqueta, alfombrado	6
cash	efectivo	16
cathode	cátodo	8
catode	cátodo	9
CD player	(el) reproductor de CDs	10
cell	celda	10
cell phone	(el) celular, (el) móvil	10
cellular	(el) celular, (el) móvil	16
cement	cemento	7
cement block	(el) bloque de cemento	7
cement mortar	mortero de cemento	7
cement render	enfoscado/ guarnecido	7
center	centro	15
centimeter	centímetro	2
ceramic product	cerámica	7
chain	cadena	12
chain saw	motosierra	12
chair	silla	16
change order	(la) orden de cambio	14
chassis, frame	(el) chasis, (el) armazón	12
cheap, unexpensive	barato	17
chemical	producto químico	7
chemical engineering	ingeniería química	3

English	Spanish	Chapter
chemistry	química	3
chief	(el/la) jefe	16
chimney	chimenea	11
chip socket	zócalo	9
cilindrical	cilíndrico	17
cinema	(el) cine	16
circle	círculo	15
circuit	circuito	8
circuit breaker (c.b.)	(el) (interruptor) magnetotérmico	8
circular	circular	17
circular saw	(la) radial	12
circular sector	(el) sector circular	15
circumference	circunferencia	15
civil engineering	ingeniería civil, de caminos	3
clay	arcilla, barro	7
client	(el/ la) cliente	4
clock	(el) reloj	16
clock signal	(la) señal de reloj	9
clutch	(el) embrague	12
CMOS	(el) CMOS (ce-mos)	9
coal	(el) carbón	7
coat	capa	6
coat	abrigo	16
cobblestone	(el) adoquín	7
coefficient	(el) coeficiente	15
cold	frío	11
collection	cobro	14
collector	(el) colector	9
colorful	de colores	17
column	columna	6
column	columna	10
combustion chamber	cámara de combustión	12
comma (1,000),	coma	15
committee	(el) comité	13
company	empresa	14

English	Spanish	Chapter
competitor	competidor/a	4
complex number	número complejo	15
component	(el) componente	8
compound	compuesto	7
compressor	(el) compresor	11
computer	(el) ordenador, (el/la) computador/a	10
computer	(el) ordenador, (el/la) computador/a	16
concept	concepto	8
concept	concepto	9
concept	concepto	10
concept	concepto	15
concept	concepto	11
concrete	(el) hormigón, concreto	7
concrete block	(el) bloque de hormigón	7
concrete slab	forjado	6
condenser	(el) condensador	11
conductance	(la) conductancia	8
conductivity	conductividad	8
cone	cono	15
configuration	(la) configuración	10
conical	cónico	17
constant	(la) constante	15
construction	(la) construcción	5
construction	(la) construcción	6
construction	(la) construcción	13
construction site	obra	6
construction site	obra	13
construction works	obra	6
construction works	obra	13
constructive	constructivo	17
consultant	consultor/a	4
consumption	consumo	8
content	contenido	10
contest	concurso	14
contingency	contingencia	13

English	Spanish	Chapter
contract	contrato	13
contractor	(el/ la) contratista	4
contractual	contractual	17
control	(el) control	9
controller	(el) regulador	9
conversation	(la) conversación	13
cooling tower	(la) torre de refrigeración	11
coordination	(la) coordinación	13
coordinator	coordinador/a	4
correlation	(la) correlación	15
corridor, landing	(el) corredor, pasillo	5
cosecant	(la) cosecante	15
cosine	coseno	15
cost	(el) coste	13
cost	(el) coste	14
cotangent	cotangente	15
covariance	(la) covarianza	15
coverage	cobertura	16
coworker	(el/la) compañero/a	16
CPU	(el) CPU (ce-pe-u)	9
crane	grúa, pluma	12
crank(shaft)	(el) cigüeñal	12
credit card	tarjeta de crédito	16
crown molding	rodatecho	6
cube	cubo	15
cube root	(la) raíz cúbica	15
cubic meter	metro cúbico	2
currency	moneda	16
current intensity	(la) corriente, (la) intensidad	8
curve	curva	15
curved	curvo	17
customer	(el) cliente	16
customs	aduana	16
cutoff	(el) corte	15
cutting point	punto de corte	15

English	Spanish	Chapter
cycle	ciclo	15
cylinder	cilindro	12
cylinder	cilindro	15
dam	presa, represa	5
dark red	rojo oscuro	17
database	(la) base de datos	10
datum, data	dato, (los) datos	10
DC	(la) corriente continua	8
deal	trato	14
dealer, salesman, vendor	(el) comercial, (el) vendedor	14
debt	deuda	14
decibel	decibelio	2
decimal	número decimal	15
decimal logarithm	logaritmo decimal	15
degree	grado	2
degree Celsius	grado Celsius	2
degree Fahrenheit	grado Fahrenheit	2
delivery term	plazo de entrega	14
demand	demanda	8
demolition	(la) demolición	6
density	(la) densidad	11
department	departamento	13
deposit	depósito	12
derivative	derivada	15
design	diseño	13
designer	diseñador/a	4
desk	escritorio, mesa	16
detail drawing	plano de detalle	6
detector	(el) detector	9
determinant	(el) determinante	15
device	dispositivo	8
device	dispositivo	9
device	dispositivo	10
device	dispositivo	11

English	Spanish	Chapter
diagram	(el) diagrama	13
diameter	diametro	15
diesel fuel	gasóleo	7
diesel generator set	grupo electrógeno	6
differential equation	(la) ecuación diferencial	15
dimension	(la) dimensión	15
dinner	cena	16
diode	diodo	9
director	director/a	4
discount	descuento	14
disk	disco	10
ditch	zanja	6
division	(la) división	13
division	(la) división	15
doctor	médico	16
document	documento	13
document	documento	16
domestic	nacional	17
door	puerta	6
door	puerta	16
double	doble	17
double integral	(la) integral doble	15
draft	(el) borrador	13
draft	borrador	17
draftsman	(el/ la) delineante, (el/ la) proyectista	4
drain	(el) drenador	9
drainage	(el) desagüe, sumidero	11
drainpipe	(la) bajante	6
drawing, blueprint	plano	6
drill	taladradora, taladro	12
drill bit	broca, barrena	12
drink	bebida	16
driver	(el) driver	10
driving carner	(el) carnet de conducir	16

English	Spanish	Chapter
duct	conducto	11
dust	polvo	7
DVD	(el) DVD (de-be-de)	10
e, 2.81…	e	15
earth, ground	tierra	8
earthing electrode	electrodo, pica de tierra	8
earthworks	movimiento de tierras	6
electric charge	carga eléctrica	8
electric field	campo eléctrico	8
electrical	eléctrico	17
electrical engineering	ingeniería eléctrica	3
electrical panel	cuadro eléctrico	8
electrician	(el/ la) electricista	4
electricity	(la) electricidad	8
electrode	electrodo	8
electron	(el) electrón	9
electronic	electrónico	17
electronic engineering	ingeniería electrónica	3
Electronics	Electrónica	9
element	elemento	7
elevation	alzado	6
elevation	alzado	6
ellipse	(la) elipse	15
email	(el) *email*, correo electrónico	10
email	(el) *email*	16
email message	(el) *email*	13
emergency	emergencia	13
emitter	(el) emisor	9
employee	empleado/a	4
employee	empleado	16
encryption	(la) encriptación	10
energy	(la) energía	8
energy	energía	11
engineer	ingeniero/a	4
engineering	ingeniería	3

English	Spanish	Chapter
enthalpy	entalpía	11
entropy	entropía	11
entry	partida	14
entry, vestibule	entrada, vestíbulo	5
environmental	medioambiental	17
equation	(la) ecuación	15
esparto	esparto	7
estimate	estimado	14
evaporator	(el) evaporador	11
exhaust	tubo de escape	12
expansion joint	junta de dilatación	6
expensive	caro	17
experiment	experimento	13
exponential	(la) exponencial	15
extractor	(el) extractor	11
facade	fachada	6
face	cara	15
facebook	(el) facebook	10
factor	(el) factor	15
factory	fábrica	5
false ceiling	falso techo	6
fan	(el) ventilador	11
fan-coil	(el) fan-coil	11
farad	faradio	2
fastener	elemento de unión	12
fax	(el) fax	10
fax message	(el) fax	13
feedback	(el) realimentación	9
fence	cerca, valla	6
fiberglass	fibra de vidrio	7
figure	cifra	15
file	archivo	16
lime	lima	12
filter	filtro	12
final	final	17

English	Spanish	Chapter
finance	(las) finanzas	14
financial	financiero	17
finishing	acabado	6
finite-state machine	máquina de estado	9
fire	incendio	11
fire extinguisher	(el) extintor	11
fire fighters	bomberos	16
fire safety	(la) seguridad contra incendios	11
fireplace	chimenea	11
first floor	(el) primer piso	5
first payment	entrada	14
fiscal	fiscal	17
flash drive, pen drive	(el) lápiz de memoria	10
flat-blade screwdriver	(el) destornillador plano	12
flight	vuelo	16
floor	suelo	6
floor tile	baldosa	7
floor, story	planta, piso	5
flow	(el) caudal, flujo	11
fluid	fluido	7
foam	espuma	7
focus	foco	15
folder	carpeta	16
follow-up	seguimiento	13
food	comida	16
force	fuerza	6
foreman	(el/ la) capataz	4
form	forma	15
formica	formica	7
formulae	fórmula	15
foton	(el) fotón	9
foundations	(los) cimientos	6
fraction	(la) fracción	15
frame	marco	6
freeway, highway	autopista	5

English	Spanish	Chapter
freeway, highway	autopista	16
frequency	frecuencia	15
front yard	patio de delante	5
function	(la) función	15
furniture	mobiliario	6
gas	(el) gas	7
gas constant (R)	constante de los gases	11
gas main	acometida de gas	11
gas meter	(el) contador de gas	11
gasket	junta	12
gasoline	gasolina	7
gate	puerta	6
gate, logic gate	puerta lógica	9
gear	(el) engranaje, marcha	12
gel	(el) gel	7
generator	(el) generador	8
generatrix	(la) generatriz	15
geometry	geometría	15
GigaBite	Gigabyte	2
glass	vidrio	7
glasses	(las) gafas	11
glasses, spectacles	(las) gafas, (los) lentes	16
gloves	(los) guantes	11
glue	pegamento	7
gram	gramo	2
graph	gráfico	15
graphic	gráfico	10
gravel	grava	7
gray	gris	17
green	verde	17
ground floor	bajo, planta baja	5
gutter	canaleta	6
gypsum	(el) mineral de yeso	7
hammer	martillo	12
handrail	barandilla	6

English	Spanish	Chapter
hard disk	disco duro	10
hardhat	(el) casco	11
hardware	(el) *hardware*	10
hardware	(el) *hardware*	10
harmonic	armónico	8
harness	(el) arnés	11
headphones	(los) auriculares	10
headquarters	(la) sede, (la) central	16
heat	(el) calor	11
heat capacity	(la) capacidad calorífica	11
heater	(el) calentador	11
height	altura	15
henry	henrio (*3)	2
hertz	hercio (*3)	2
hidrant	(el) hidrante	11
hinge	bisagra	12
hole	agujero	6
hole	hueco	9
hollow	hueco	6
hook	gancho	12
hopper	tolva	12
hose	manguera	11
hospital	(el) hospital	16
hotel	(el) hotel	16
house	casa	5
human resources	(los) recursos humanos	13
humidity	(la) humedad	11
hydraulic	hidráulico	17
hydrogen	hidrógeno	7
hyperbolic cosecant	(la) cosecante hiperbólica	15
hyperbolic cosine	coseno hiperbólico	15
hyperbolic cotangent	(la) cotangente hiperbólica	15
hyperbolic secant	(la) secante hiperbólica	15
hyperbolic sine	seno hiperbólico	15
hyperbolic tangent	(la) tangente hiperbólica	15

English	Spanish	Chapter
ice	hielo	7
imaginary number	número imaginario	15
impedance	impedancia	8
impedance	impedancia	8
in trial	en pruebas	17
in warranty	en garantía	17
individual	individual	17
inductance, coil	inductancia, bobina	8
inductor	bovina, (el) inductor	8
industrial building	(la) nave industrial	5
industry	industria	5
inequality	(la) inecuación	15
infinite	infinito	15
infinitesimal	infinitésimo	15
inflection point	punto de inflexión	15
inspection	(la) inspección	13
inspector	inspector/a	4
instructions	(las) instrucciones	13
insulator	aislamiento, (el) aislante	8
insurance	seguro	13
insurance	seguro, seguranza	16
integer number	número entero	15
integral	(la) integral	15
internal energy	energía interna	11
international	internacional	17
internet conection	(la) conexión de internet	16
inverter	(el) inversor	9
investment	(la) inversión	14
iron	hierro	7
irrational number	número irracional	15
jack	gato	12
Java	Java	10
job	trabajo	13
joint	(la) articulación	12
joule	julio	2

English	Spanish	Chapter
junction box	caja de derivación	8
kelvin	(el) kelvin, grado kelvin	2
key	(la) llave	16
keyboard	teclado	10
kilo (kilogram)	kilo (kilogramo)	2
kilowatt hour	kilovatio hora	2
kitchen	cocina	5
lab gown	bata	11
laboratory	laboratorio	13
ladder	escalera	12
land	tierra	6
language	(el) lenguaje	10
Laplace transform	transformada de Laplace	9
laptop	(el) portátil	10
laser	(el) láser	8
law	(la) ley	13
layout, floor plan	planta, (el) layout	5
layout, floor plan	planta, (el) layout	6
lease	(el) lease	14
LED (light emitting diode)	(el) LED (led)	9
legal	legal	17
length	(la) longitud	15
letter	carta	13
letter of intent	carta de intención	13
level	(el) nivel	6
lever	palanca	12
liability	pasivo	14
license	licencia	13
lift shaft	hueco del ascensor	5
light bulb	bombilla, bombillo	8
light fixture	luminaria	8
light red	rojo claro	17
lighting	(la) iluminación	8
lighting circuit	circuito de alumbrado	8
lightning rod	(el) parrayos	8

English	Spanish	Chapter
lime	(la) cal	7
lime mortar	mortero de cal, argamasa	7
limestone	roca caliza	7
limit	(el) límite	15
line	línea	15
line	recta	15
linea, wire	línea, hilo	8
linear, first-degree	lineal, de primer grado	17
link	(el) eslabón	12
lintel	(el) dintel	6
liquid	líquido	7
list	lista	10
liter	litro	2
living room, dining room	(el) cuarto de estar, (el) comedor	5
load (power)	carga (eléctrica)	8
load (structural load)	carga	6
load-bearing wall	muro de carga	6
loan	préstamo	14
local	local	17
logarithm	logaritmo	15
logic family	familia lógica	9
long-term	a largo plazo	17
loop	(el) bucle	9
loss	pérdida	8
lost	pérdida	14
lot	(el) área	5
lubricant	(el) lubricante	7
luggage	(el) equipaje	16
lump item	partida alzada	14
machine tool	máquina herramienta	12
machinery	maquinaria	12
magnetic field	campo magnético	8
magnetic field B	campo magnético B	8
magnetic field H	campo magnético H	8
magnetic flux	flujo (magnético)	8

English	Spanish	Chapter
magnetic reluctance	(la) reluctancia (magnética)	8
main	acometida	8
maintenance	mantenimiento	13
management	(la) dirección, (la) gestión	13
manager	director/a	4
manhole	boca de alcantarilla	11
manual	(el) manual	13
manual	(el) manual	17
map	(el) mapa	13
marketing	mercadotécnia, (el) *marketing*	3
mass	masa	11
material	(el) material	7
mathematics	(las) matemáticas	3
mathematics	(las) matemáticas	15
matrix	(la) matriz	15
maximum	máximo	15
measurement	(la) medición	14
measuring instrument	aparato de medida	8
mechanical	mecánico/a	4
mechanical	mecánico	17
mechanical engineering	ingeniería mecánica	3
medicine	medicina	16
meeting	(la) reunión	13
meeting room	sala de reunión	16
MegaByte	*Megabyte*	2
memory	memoria	10
memory card	tarjeta de memoria	10
menu	(el) menú	10
menu	(el) menú	16
message	(el) mensaje, (la) comunicación	13
meter	(el) contador, (el) medidor	8
meter per second	metro por segundo	2
meter per second squared	metro por segundo al cuadrado	2
method	método	13
method of payment	forma de pago	14

English	Spanish	Chapter
metro	metro	2
mezanine	(el) *mezanine*, entreplanta	5
microchip, integrated circuit	(el) chip, circuito integrado	9
microcontroller	(el) microcontrolador	9
microphone	micrófono	10
microprocessor	(el) microprocesador	9
milimeter	milímetro	2
milling machine	fresadora	12
mineral	(el) mineral	7
minimum	mínimo	15
miscellaneous	misceláneo	6
mixture	mezcla	7
modem	(el) módem	10
money	dinero	14
monitor	(el) monitor	10
mortar	mortero	7
mortgage	hipoteca	14
motor	(el) motor	8
motor	(el) motor	12
mouse	(el) ratón	10
move	mudanza	6
move	mudanza	13
mud	barro	7
multimeter	multímetro	8
multiple	múltiple	17
multiplication	producto	15
n MOSFET	(el) MOSFET de canal n	9
nail	clavo	12
natural	natural	17
natural gas	(el) gas natural	7
natural logarithm (Naperian)	logaritmo neperiano	15
natural number	número natural	15
natural product	producto natural	7
naval architecture	ingeniería naval	3

English	Spanish	Chapter
negative number	número negativo	15
negotiation	(la) negociación	14
network	(la) red	10
neutral	neutro	8
new, brand-new	nuevo	17
news	(las) noticias	16
newspaper	periódico	16
newton	(el) newton (*4)	2
nitrogen	nitrógeno	7
norm	norma	13
normal distribution	(la) distribución normal	15
npn BJT	(el) transistor NPN (ene-pe-ene)	9
nuclear	nuclear	17
nuclear power plan	(la) central nuclear	5
number	número	15
numerical control m.	máquina de control numérico	12
nut	tuerca	12
offer	oferta	14
office	oficina	16
office building	edificio de oficinas	5
ohm	ohmio	2
oil	(el) aceite	7
oil (petroleum)	petróleo	7
open area	(el) área abierta	5
open circuit	circuito abierto	8
openwork wall	muro palomero	6
operation	(la) operación	13
operation	(la) operación	15
operational amplifier	(el) amplificador operacional	9
orange	naranja	17
order of magnitude	(la) orden de magnitud	15
organization	(la) organización	13
oscilloscope	osciloscopio	8
outlet	(el) enchufe	8
oval	óvalo	15

English	Spanish	Chapter
overall	mono, (el) overol	11
overhead	(los) gastos generales	14
overload	sobrecarga	8
owned	en propiedad	17
oxide	óxido	7
oxygen	oxígeno	7
p MOSFET	(el) MOSFET de canal p	9
package	cápsula	9
page	página	10
paint	pintura	7
panic bar, crash bar	barra antipánico	11
paper	(el) papel	16
parallel	en paralelo	17
parameter	parámetro	15
parapet	peto	6
parcel of land	parcela	5
park	(el) parque	5
parking area	estacionamiento	5
parking building	edificio de aparcamientos	5
parking lot	aparcamiento al aire libre	5
parquet floor	parqué	6
part	pieza	12
partition	(el) tabique	6
pascal	(el) pascal	2
pass	(el) pase, (la) autorización	16
passport	(el) pasaporte	16
pasta	pasta	7
path	camino, sendero	5
pay off	finiquito	14
payment, installment	pago, letra	14
pen	bolígrafo	16
percentage	(el) porcentaje	15
period	periodo	15
personal	personal	17
phase	(la) fase	8

English	Spanish	Chapter
phase	(la) fase	13
Phillip screwdriver	(el) destornillador de estrella	12
phone	teléfono	10
photo	(la) foto	16
photodiode	fotodiodo	9
physics	física	3
pi, π	(el) pi	15
pickaxe	pico	12
PID controller	(el) regulador PID (pe-i-de)	9
piecework	a destajo	17
pillar	(el) pilar	6
pin	(el) pin, patilla	9
pipe	tubería	11
piston	(el) pistón	12
plan	(el) plan	13
plane	plano	15
plane	(el) avión	16
planning	(la) planificación	13
plant	planta	6
plaster	revoco (4)	7
plaster (material)	yeso	7
plastic	plástico	7
pliers	(los) alicates	12
plug	(el) enchufe (macho), clavija	8
plug	bujía	12
plumb-bob, plummet	plomada	6
plumber	fontanero/a, plomero/a	4
PN junction	(la) unión PN (pe-ene)	9
pneumatic	pneumatico	17
pnp BJT	(el) transistor PNP (pe-ene-pe)	9
point (period 2.3)	punto	15
point, dot	punto	15
pole	polo	15
police	policia	16
porch	(el) porche	5

English	Spanish	Chapter
port	puerto	5
port	puerto	9
position	puesto	4
potentiometer	potenciómetro	8
powder	polvo	7
power	potencia	8
power	potencia	11
power	potencia	15
power 2, square	cuadrado	15
power 3, cube	cubo	15
power circuit	circuito de fuerza	8
power factor, cos φ	(el) factor de potencia	8
power plant	(la) central de energía	5
power supply	(la) fuente de alimentación	8
preasure	(la) presión	11
president	presidente/a	4
pressure	(la) presión	6
price	precio	14
primatic	primático	17
printer	impresora	10
prism	(el) prisma	15
probe	sonda	13
procedure	procedimiento	13
process	proceso	13
Procurement, Purchasing	(las) compras	14
product	producto	7
product	producto	13
production	(la) producción	13
professional	(el/ la) profesional	4
professional	profesional	17
profit	ganancia	14
program	(el) programa	10
program	(el) programa	13
project	proyecto	13
project coordinator	coordinador/a de proyectos	4

English	Spanish	Chapter
project management	(la) dirección de proyectos	3
project management	(la) dirección de proyectos	13
project manager	director/a de proyectos	4
propeller	(la) hélice	12
proportion	(la) proporción	15
protection	(la) protección	11
protocole	(el) protocolo	10
provisional	provisional	17
psychrometric chart	(el) diagrama psicrométrico	11
pull station	alarma de incendio	11
pulley	polea	12
pump	bomba	11
purchase	compra	14
purchase order	(la) orden de compra	14
PVC	(el) PVC (pe uve ce)	7
quadrant	(el) cuadrante	15
quadratic, second-degree	cuadrático, de segundo grado	17
quality	(la) calidad	13
quality	de calidad	17
quantity	(la) magnitud	8
quantity	(la) magnitud	11
quicklime	(la) cal viva	7
radian	(el) radián	2
radiator	(el) radiador	11
radiator	(el) radiador	12
radio	(el) radio, (la) radio	16
radius	radio	15
raised floor	falso suelo	6
ramp	rampa	5
ratio	ratio	15
raw material	materia prima	7
reactive power	potencia reactiva	8
real estate	(los) inmuebles, bienes raíces	14
real number	número real	15
real power	potencia activa	8

English	Spanish	Chapter
receipt	recibo	14
recepcionist	(el/la) recepcionista	16
rectangle	rectángulo	15
rectangular	rectangular	17
rectifier	(el) rectificador	8
red	rojo	17
regulation	(la) regulación	13
regulatory	reglamentario	17
reinforced concrete	(el) hormigón armado	7
relative humidity	(la) humedad relativa	11
relocation	(la) reubicación	13
rendering	revestimiento	7
rent	(el) alquiler	14
rental	en alquiler, de alquiler	17
reset signal	(la) señal de reset	9
residual value	(el) valor residual	14
residual-current c.b.	(el) (interruptor) diferencial	8
resistance	resistencia	8
resistivity	(la) resistividad	8
resistor	resistencia	8
restaurant	(el) restaurante	16
restrooms	(los) aseos, (los) baños	5
rev. per second	(la) revolución por segundo	2
revision	(la) revisión	13
ring-shaped	con forma de anillo	17
riser shaft	patinillo de instalaciones	5
rivet	(el) remache	12
road (car road)	carretera	5
robot	(el) robot	9
rock	roca	7
roof	techo	5
roof	cubierta	6
roof tile	teja	7
room	cuarto, sala, pieza	5
room	(la) habitación	16

English	Spanish	Chapter
root	(la) raíz	15
rope	cuerda	12
row	fila	10
rule	regla	13
rules	reglamento	13
S transform	transformada en s (ese)	9
sale	venta	14
salt	(la) sal	7
sample	muestra	13
sand	arena	7
sanitary how water	(el) agua caliente sanitaria	11
satellite	(el) satélite	9
savings	ahorro	14
saw	sierra	12
sawdust	(el) serrín	7
scaffold	andamio	6
scaffolding	(el) andamiaje	6
scalar	(el) escalar	15
scanner	(el) escáner	10
schedule	agenda, (el) programa	16
science	ciencia	3
scope of services	(el) alcance de los servicios	14
screw	tornillo de punta	12
screwdriver	(el) destornillador	12
secant	(la) secante	15
second	segundo	2
second derivative	segunda derivada	15
secondhand	de segunda mano	17
secretary	(el/la) secretario/a	16
section	(la) sección	13
section	sección	15
section drawing	sección	6
security	(la) seguridad	13
security deposit	depósito de seguridad	14
segment	segmento	15

English	Spanish	Chapter
seller	(el) vendedor	14
semicircle	semicírculo	15
semiconductor	(el) semiconductor	9
sensor	(el) sensor	9
sensor	(el) sensor	11
septic tank	fosa séptica	11
sequence	secuencia	13
series	en serie	17
server	(el) servidor	10
set	conjunto	13
sewer	alcantarilla	11
sewer system	(la) red de alcantarillas	11
sewerage	(las) aguas residuales	11
sheet	plancha, chapa	6
sheet rock	Pladur®, placa de yeso	7
shop	tienda	16
short circuit	cortocircuito	8
short-term	a corto plazo	17
shunt	(el) *shunt*, (la) derivación	8
side	lado	15
signal	(la) señal	9
simple	simple	17
sine	seno	15
single family dwelling	(el) chalet, casa	5
sink	pila	11
sinusoid	(el) senoide	15
site manager	jefe/a de obra	4
sketch	(el) croquis, dibujo	6
skylight	lucernario	6
slaked lime	(la) cal apagada, cal muerta	7
smoke	humo	11
smoke detector	(el) detector de humos	11
socket	(el) enchufe, toma de corriente	8
software	(el) *software*	10
software	informatico, de *software*	17

English	Spanish	Chapter
software engineering	informática	3
solar	solar	17
solid	sólido	7
solid angle	ángulo sólido	15
sound card	tarjeta de sonido	10
source	(la)fuente	9
speaker	(el) altavoz	10
specialist	especialista	4
specific heat capacity	(el) calor especifico	11
sphere	esfera	15
spherical	esférico	17
spreadsheet	hoja de cálculo	10
spring	(el) muelle, (el) resorte	12
sprinkler	(el) sprinkler	11
square	cuadrado	15
square meter	metro cuadrado	2
square root	(la) raíz cuadrada	15
squared	cuadrado	17
stairs	escalera	5
standard	estándar	17
station (bus, train)	(la) estación	16
statistical	estadística	15
steady state	(el) régimen permanente	9
steel	acero	7
steering wheel	(el) volante	12
step	(el) escalón	6
stick (wooden)	palo	12
stock	(el) stock , (el) almacén	14
stone	piedra	7
stonework	fábrica de piedra	7
straight	recto	17
street	(la) calle	5
street	(la) calle	16
street map	plano	16
structure	estructura	6

English	Spanish	Chapter
substation	(la) subestación	8
subtraction	resta	15
suit	(el) traje	16
sum, summation, addition	suma	15
supply	suministro	8
switch	(el) interruptor	8
symbol	símbolo	10
symbol	símbolo	15
system	(el) sistema	13
table	tabla	10
tablet, ipad	tableta, (el) *ipad*	10
tangent	(la) tangente	15
tank	(el) tanque, depósito	11
tank	(el) tanque	12
tap	grifo	11
tape measure	cinta métrica	12
task	tarea	13
taxes	(los) impuestos	14
taxi	(el) taxi	16
Taylor series	(la) serie de *Taylor*	15
team	equipo	13
technical	técnico	17
technical specialties	(las) especialidades ténicas	
technician	(el/ la) técnico	4
technology	tecnología	3
television	(la) televisión	16
temperature	temperatura	11
temporary	temporal	17
term	plazo	13
terminal	(el) terminal	9
terrace, balcon	terraza, (el) balcón	5
terracotta	terracota	7
test	(el) test	13
test tube	probeta	13
thermal	térmico	17

English	Spanish	Chapter
thermic load	carga (térmica)	11
thermistor	(el) termistor	9
thermocouple	(el) termopar	9
thermodinamics	termodinámica	11
thermostat	termostato	11
Thevenin equivalent	(el) equivalente Thévenin	8
ticket	(el) billete, (el) tiquet	16
timetable	calendario, horario	16
tire	neumático	12
toilet	inodoro	11
tongs	(las) tenazas	12
tonne	tonelada	2
tool	heramienta	12
tooth	(el) diente	12
topography engineering	ingeniería de topografía	3
torque	(el) par	6
town hall	ayuntamiento	16
train	(el) tren	16
tranparent	tranparente	17
transducer	(el) trasductor	9
transform	transformada	15
transformer	(el) transformador	8
transient event	(el) régimen transitorio	9
transistor	(el) transistor	9
transport	(el) transporte	13
transportation	(el) transporte	16
travel	(el) viaje	16
tread	rodamiento	12
triangle	triángulo	15
triangular	triangular	17
trigonometry	trigonometría	15
triple integral	(la) integral triple	15
trowel	llana	6
truss	cercha	6
truth table	tabla de verdad	9

English	Spanish	Chapter
TTL	(el) TTL (te-te-ele)	9
turbine	turbina	11
turn-key	llave en mano	17
twit, twiter	(el) *twit*, (el) *twiter*	10
tyristor	(el) tiristor	9
underground, subway	metro	16
unforeseen	(el) imprevisto	13
unit	(la) unidad	2
unit	(la) unidad	14
unit price	(el) precio unitario	14
unknown	incógnita	15
UPS	UPS (u-pe-ese), SAI (sai)	8
utility room	cuarto de servicio	5
value	(el) valor	14
valve	válvula	11
valve	válvula	12
variable	(la) variable	15
variance	varianza	15
VAT	Impuesto del Valor Añadido	14
vault	bóveda	6
vector	(el) vector	15
vendor	vendedor/a, (el/ la) comercial	4
ventilation grate	rejilla	11
vertex	(el) vértice	15
video	vídeo, video	16
video camera	cámara de vídeo	10
video card	tarjeta de vídeo	10
video conference	videoconferencia	13
violet	violeta	17
virus	(el) virus	10
volt	voltio	2
voltage drop	caída de tensión	8
voltage, tension	(el) voltaje, (la) tensión	8
voltmeter	voltímetro	8
volume	(el) volumen	11

English	Spanish	Chapter
work	trabajo	16
work (as in brickwork)	fábrica	7
work of art	obra de arte	13
work phone	teléfono en el trabajo	16
work shed	caseta de obra	6
work, effort	trabajo	13
worker	trabajador/a	4
workshop	(el) taller	5
wrench, spanner	(la) llave	12
yard, patio	patio	5
yellow	amarillo	17
Z transform	transformada en z (zeta)	9
ZIP	código postal	16

USING ENGLISH TO LEARN SPANISH
BOOKS OF THE SERIES

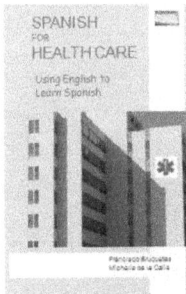

SPANISH FOR HEALTH CARE

Spanish for the Health Care is intended **for professionals** with no previous knowledge of Spanish. **The goal is to communicate with patients**. The book focuses on the dialogue to understand symptoms, and convey diagnostics and instructions.

The right way for professionals to learn Spanish is to learn the Spanish of the profession.

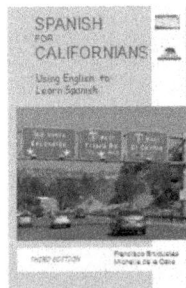

SPANISH FOR ENGINEERS

Spanish for the Engineers is intended **for professionals** with no previous knowledge of Spanish. **The goal is to communicate in your technical environment**. Each chapter focuses on one specialty, including construction, software, M&E engineering and project management.

The right way for professionals to learn Spanish is to learn the Spanish of the profession.

SPANISH FOR CALIFORNIANS

Spanish for Californians shows the Spanish of **Latin America and the U.S.** One of the twenty-two Academies that represent Spanish is in the U.S. The book teaches the common within the norm.

A textbook for beginners, and a reference data book for speakers. The easiest way to learn is by learning the simplest first.

ADVANCED SPANISH

Advanced Spanish focuses on **those topics that are an obstacle for your fluent Spanish**. The textbook explains the subjects with many examples and comparisons to English.

Now that you can communicate, it is time to get to the point and perfect your Spanish.